Pennsylvania
Blue-Ribbon
Fly-Fishing Guide

BARRY & CATHY BECK

Pennsylvania
Blue-Ribbon
Fly-Fishing Guide

BARRY & CATHY BECK

Biography

Barry and Cathy Beck live in the Fishing Creek Valley in northeastern Pennsylvania. In addition to their writing and photography, the Beck's host fly-fishing trips for Frontiers, International, are members of the Sage Fly Fishing Team, instruct fly-fishing schools, and give fly-fishing presentations. Their other books are, *Cathy Beck's Fly Fishing Handbook*, *Seasons of the Bighorn*, and *Fly Fishing the Flats.*

Dedication

This book is dedicated to the Pennsylvania chapters of Trout Unlimited and local conservation clubs, like our own Freestone Fly Fishers and the Fishing Creek Watershed Association. The efforts of these clubs working with the Pennsylvania Fish & Boat Commission will ensure the future of our fisheries.

Photography: Barry & Cathy Beck unless otherwise noted.
Fly Plate Photography: Jim Schollmeyer
Design: Jerry Hutchinson

Softbound ISBN: 1-57188-158-1
Softbound UPC: 0-66066-00356-0

Frank Amato Publications, Inc.
P.O. Box 82112, Portland, Oregon 97282
(503) 653-8108
Printed in Hong Kong
1 3 5 7 9 10 8 6 4 2

P E N N S Y L V A N I A

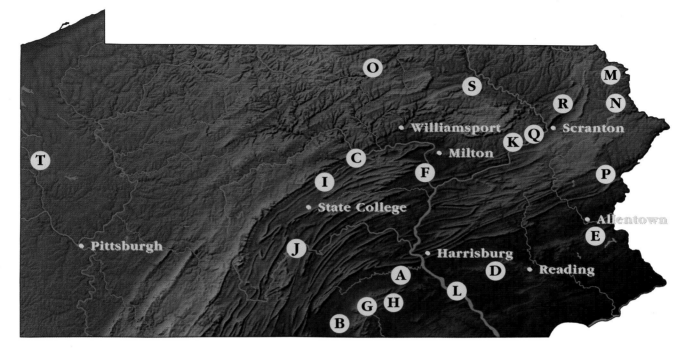

T A B L E O F C O N T E N T S

Introduction
Pennsylvania Fly Water

As you enter Pennsylvania, the sign says Welcome to Pennsylvania, America Starts Here. History tells us that fly-fishing in this country started here, too. Fly-fishing as we know it today has roots firmly planted in the Pocono Mountains of the Keystone State.

With over 10,000 miles of trout streams, numerous lakes and ponds and over 100 miles of the Susquehanna River, possibly the best smallmouth bass water in the entire Northeast, Pennsylvania has a lot to offer the fly-fisherman.

The diversity of the trout water alone is impressive and includes anything from remote backcountry brook trout streams to the historic limestone streams known to trout anglers throughout the world. Another plus is the amount of regulated water that the Pennsylvania Fish Commission offers from Fly–Fishing–Only projects to the popular Delayed Harvest areas. Tailwater fisheries like the Delaware mimic their counterparts of the West and freestone trout streams abound almost everywhere in the state.

Along with the coldwater rivers and streams, the state also has a trout-stocking program aimed at the many coldwater lakes that are available. So if trout is your game, Pennsylvania's your playing field.

It may be hard to believe but the Susquehanna River at 444 miles is the longest non-navigable river in North America. For the smallmouth bass enthusiast in Pennsylvania, the opportunities are endless especially since much of the river is very accessible to the public and easy to wade because of shallow depths. Warmwater lakes and ponds throughout the state offer fly-fishing for bass and panfish and many are owned and maintained by the Pennsylvania Fish Commission.

History also tells us that our state has given our sport some of the best of our fly-fishing writers and personalities. The late Vincent Marinaro and Charles Fox were legendary anglers and authors from the famed Cumberland Valley and the Letort Spring Run. Their contributions to tying and fishing with terrestrial fly patterns opened new horizons to trout fishermen everywhere. Charles Wetzel, once considered the dean of Penns Creek, left us with his *Practical Fly Fishing*, Alvin Grove his *Lure and Lore of Trout Fishing* and perhaps no one has influenced Pennsylvania anglers more than George Harvey of Penn State fame. Ed Shenk published his *Fly Rod Trouting* in 1989 and Ed Jaworowski has given us an excellent casting book in *The Cast*. The literary list goes on with Charles Meck and Dwight Landis who share their enthusiasm and who through their work have helped countless numbers of anglers to find their way around the trout streams of Pennsylvania.

Our cabin home is located in the Endless Mountain Region of the state and a short 10-minute drive from Fishing Creek, our home stream. From the front porch we can see the spring head of Raven Creek, a tributary to Fishing Creek that has a native brook trout population, along with the spring head is Campbell's Pond full of panfish and bass. Behind the cabin and a short walk through the woods is Yurch's Pond, another good spot for bass and panfish. Looking east is Kitchen and Huntington, two more wild brook and brown trout fisheries. We are in a sense surrounded by water and it's one of the many reasons that Pennsylvania is so special to us.

We spend a good deal of our time writing, photographing and hosting fishing trips. Our work takes us around the world to some very unique fishing destinations and we could live almost anywhere, but there is always something that brings us back to these mountains in northeastern Pennsylvania, it's a good place to call home.

This book is by no means a complete guide to all that our state has to offer in the way of fishing. Instead it represents the answers to our most often asked questions of where do we like to fish at home and what our favorite fish are. Honestly, we like it all, so it's a hard questions to answer. We're as happy on a panfish pond as we are on a trout stream. Put simply, we like to fly-fish and perhaps the best part is just being there-wherever "there" is. This book is a collection of trout, bass and some panfish destinations that we visit as often as we can and I guess that makes them our favorites.

Most trout fishermen are familiar with the limestone trout streams of Pennsylvania and that's where our book starts. These streams are often described as the jewels of our state and they are truly blue-ribbon waters. Born generally in large spring heads, these limestone streams are high in alkalinity and combined with cold water year round, water temperatures and flows vary little helping to create the perfect environment in which a trout can live. The meadows of the fabled Letort Spring Run, Big Springs and Falling Springs are often compared to the English chalk streams where weed-choked currents and minute insects bring ultra-selective trout to the surface.

Penns Creek, Big Fishing Creek and the Yellow Breeches are also streams rich in alkalinity and considered to be limestone fisheries, but unlike the silty and weedy bottoms of the Letort or Big Springs, they have the composite or the riffle/pool/riffle combination associated with most freestone trout streams and rocky bottoms lack the weed growth of their meadow counterparts.

Throughout the text and images we will share with you our feelings about each piece of water, perhaps add a fishing story or two, address important insect hatches, suggest tackle ideas and whenever possible list local lodging or campgrounds. Some will include a local fly shop or contacts should you decide to visit.

If you're a resident of Pennsylvania, perhaps you'll find a new stream to visit or maybe be reminded of a stream to which you'd like to return. If you're new to Pennsylvania fly-fishing, get ready for an adventure. Our state has a lot to offer you!

The Letort

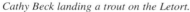

To fish the meadows section of this Cumberland Valley limestoner is to fish a piece of water rich in the history of our sport. It is truly hallowed water. Legends were born here and the best of the best have cast their offerings through the years to the finicky trout of the Letort. It was here that Marinaro and Fox made their mark in angling history and their literary works tell of serpentine bends lined with water cress and elodea. Fly patterns were developed here and tied by nimble fingers moved by creative minds and have lasted through the years. The Letort Hopper, Cricket and Beetle are as popular on western spring creeks today as they are in the pastoral valley streams of Pennsylvania. Marinaro's Jassid has found its way around the world and British anglers relay on it when the chalkstream browns are being fussy.

Pennsylvania's Cumberland Valley is rich in limestone deposits and spawns other fertile streams, but it's the Letort that stands high above the others. Weed-choked currents play havoc with 7X tippets as much today as they did when Marinaro and Fox walked these meadows. There are those

who will quickly tell you that the Letort, along with its hatches and trout, like Marinaro and Fox, are gone. While it may be true that this is not the fishery that once existed, it is still worthy of a visit not only for the fishing, but for the history itself. Barry has fished the Letort since he was a teenager and we still make an annual pilgrimage in July or August. Its cool water temperatures are welcome when most freestone trout streams in our Keystone State are suffering with low water and warm water temperatures. We never go with high expectations of fish caught even though we usually manage to fool a couple. It's difficult fishing at best, the fish are spooky and will bolt for cover at the slightest mistake by an unwary angler. Your back cast will often tangle in the bushes, and if you make the mistake of trying to wade, you can sink to your knees in muck. Summer mosquitoes will be waiting for you along with a few no-see-ums, so take insect repellent.

Presentation is as important to success on the Letort today as it was in Marinaro's time. One quickly learns to be patient. Anglers who develop a heron-like approach always

Cathy Beck landing a trout on the Letort.

A careful approach is necessary on small streams.

do better than those who plunge ahead. Cress bugs are a stable diet for Letort trout, and anglers who cast and dead drift their imitations correctly will come to know a Letort brown. Sculpins and Woolly Buggers fished deep and tight against the banks can also produce some of the largest Letort fish and Sulphur and Trico hatches still do well on certain sections of the stream. Fly boxes should obviously carry a selection of Letort Crickets, Hoppers and Beetles as well as a few ant patterns.

Tackle for fishing the Letort is up for discussion especially when it comes to rod length. Most Letort "regulars" agree on line weights of three or four. A few of the modern Letort fishermen feel that a longer rod will keep your back cast higher and out of the bushes, but the regulars like Ed Shenk will effectively fish the water with six-foot graphites.

Shenk probably knows the Letort and its trout better than anyone. We once fished the Letort with Ed and at each bend or undercut bank he would tell us the size of the trout that lived there. If we were lucky enough to catch the resident fish, it would always be exactly the fish Ed predicted.

This is hip-boot water and although you may see anglers in chest waders, the most successful fishermen rarely step into the water—and then only when it's necessary to get into position to make a cast. Barry still talks about the cast he saw Lefty Kreh make years ago on the Letort. Apparently there was a very good fish that Charlie Fox had spotted on a bend just above his house. The problem was that the fish was living under a rose

Author Charles Fox on the Letort.

bush on the far bank. In the middle of the stream was a large weed bed with a channel of water on both sides. To make matters worse, the fish was holding in slack water under the bush. The cast had to be on the money, there was no room for error.

Charlie pointed the fish out to Lefty and laughed at the impossible situation. Lefty moved into a kneeling position and made one cast. The line landed softly on the weed bed while the leader and fly drifted effortlessly into the pocket and with one

The modern-day Letort.

A low profile helps when sneaking up on the fish.

Watching for a minute can often defeat a "bank feeder"

sucking sound the trout took the fly. Nothing to it—if you're Lefty Kreh.

The Letort is easy to get to and can be reached at the Carlisle exits off Interstate 81. Lodging is convenient with numerous motels located in and around Carlisle, and at the popular Allenberry Resort on the Yellow Breeches in the village of Boiling Springs. Guiding is available through Ed Shenk at 717-243-2679, Tom Balez at Yellow Breeches Outfitters at 717-258-6752, and Cold Spring Anglers at 717-245-2646.

In the early morning hours of first light on any July or August morning, a cool mist holds above the Letort's currents. The bench that Marinaro and Fox would often share as they contemplated the day's fishing yet to come is still there. If you listen closely you may hear the echoes of times past and see the honey-

colored cane rods casting lines across currents and eddies or smell the fresh mint in the air. The sun will soon burn off the mist and the carpenter ants will find their way to the water. If you're lucky that day, you'll see and hear the sounds of a feeding Letort brown.

The Letort, starting at about 300 yards above the bridge on Township Rd. 481, downstream to the Reading Railroad bridge at the southern edge of Letort Spring Park is under a Heritage Trout Angling program managed by the Pennsylvania Fish Commission. The regulations are fly-fishing-only, all flies must be barbless. No trout may be killed and fishing hours are one hour before sunrise to one hour after sunset. The fishing on this section is open year round. A current Pennsylvania fishing license and trout stamp are required.

Falling Springs

Falling Springs was another of Vincent Marinaro's favorites. Not far from the limestone streams of Cumberland County, and one of the few streams in the state to have a population of wild rainbow trout, Falling Springs also has one of the better Trico and Sulphur hatches. This small meadow stream can offer the dry-fly purist a real challenge. Currents mix and mingle and wild trout are shy and selective requiring a serious effort on the angler's part.

It was a Sunday morning in August in the early 1970s. My old Land Rover was packed with fishing gear and my fishing companion was Marinaro. We took the Chambersburg exit off of Interstate 81 and headed for Falling Springs Road. Vince was in high spirits having just completed a new bamboo fly rod. He planned to christen the rod on the rainbow trout of Falling Springs.

The weather was perfect, no wind to speak of and a beautiful morning sunrise gave promise of things to come. There was only one other car in the parking lot which was almost unbelievable considering it was the peak of the Trico season.

Normally Vince liked to tinker with his gear, checking this and checking that as he prepared for the day's fishing, but it was clear that today he was an angler with a purpose and he wasted no time in pulling on his hip boots and stringing up the new rod. We headed upstream of the parking lot to a favorite bend pool that always held a few good trout. The first of the Trico duns appeared and like a switch turned on the trout responded.

On our knees, we eased into position. Vince pointed with his rod tip to a fish that was showing against the far bank. "Now that's a buster," Vince said. This was a frequent term that Vince put on any fish that looked big. The rainbow would show his nose as he sipped in the Trico duns and then disappear back to the bankside cover. Vince commented that this was a fish worthy of his new rod. The first cast was on the mark, the Marinaro imitation drifted down to the feeding fish. The fish came to the fly, we held our breath, and watched the inspection and the refusal. The next cast and the same scenario. A half hour passed and the game continued. Spinners were showing in the air above the water.

Fly-fishing on Falling Springs Run.

Spring creeks are fertile fisheries.

Orvis project on Falling Springs Run.

Now other fish in the pool were busy feeding but Vince stayed with the rainbow. I knew better than to suggest that he try another, it was this fish or no fish. The temptation of the feeding fish became too great and I left Vince to find one for myself. Six or seven heads were visible at the head of the run, these guys were gorging themselves on Tricos. From my position I could see they were all rainbows and not a small one in the bunch. Nervous fingers fumbled with the 6X tippet and

the size 22 Trico spinner, I double checked the clinch knot and moved closer to the edge of the water.

A final look downstream confirmed that Vince was still working on his fish, I could see the sweep of the rod tip, the loop of the fly line and then suddenly the excitement in his voice. "He's on, the buster's on." I left my rod and uncoiled fly line and ran downstream. As he extended his British landing net capturing the spent rainbow, Vince was smiling and going

Fly-fishing on Pennsylvania's Falling Springs Run.

Joe Macus fishes a cress bug imitation on Pennsylvania's Falling Springs run.

Blue-Ribbon Streams: Falling Springs

on with how well everything went after the fish finally took the fly. A quick photo and the rainbow quietly disappeared to the safety of the stream.

The cigar in Vince's mouth twirled around and I knew that I was going to hear the capture of the rainbow one more time and in its entirety. Meanwhile my fish were probably busy inhaling Trico spinners. Footsteps announced the arrival of two other anglers who it turns out were friends of Marinaro's and they too listened to the fish story. I can honestly call it a fish story because the rainbow looked to be 15 inches, but by the time the story ended it had grown to at least 19 inches. A fitting fish to christen the new rod. On that note I excused myself and headed back upstream.

Sometimes it just goes this way. I arrived back at the head of the riffle just in time to see another angler standing in my spot and landing a really nice fish. He looked up and asked if the fly rod laying on the bank belonged to me. I said that it did and complimented him on his fish. The Trico spinners were just about done, downstream Vince still had a captive audience, the morning fishing was all but over.

Falling Springs is easy to reach from the Chambersburg exit off of Interstate 81, follow Route 30 to SR2029 or Falling Spring Road which parallels most of the stream. On the stream, 2.4 miles are listed under the Heritage Trout Program and there is a 1.1-mile section of Delayed Harvest.

This is primarily hip-boot water and the most successful anglers fish from the bank. The wild fish are exactly that, wild and smart, keep a low profile and limit your number of false casts. Sulphurs, Tricos and blue-winged olives are the mainstay of the hatches, but cressbug patterns and a good selection of terrestrials should also be included. One of my best days on the water started with a heavy Trico spinner fall and ended with an 18-inch rainbow landed at dark on a size 8 Woolly Bugger.

Lodging is easily found at hotels located at the Chambersburg exits off of I-81, and there is a well-stocked fly shop (Falling Springs Outfitters) in nearby Scotland, at Exit 8. Falling Springs' future looks good thanks to the efforts of local landowners, Trout Unlimited, The Orvis Company, and the Greenway Project.

A classic piece of spring-creek water on Pennsylvania's Falling Springs Run.

Pennsylvania Blue-Ribbon Fly-Fishing Guide

Just to keep things interesting, Pennsylvania has five Fishing Creeks; four are freestone in origin and one is limestone. Of the five, two are regarded as great trout fisheries. One is a freestoner located in northeastern Pennsylvania and the other is a limestoner located in the central region of the state. It is without question the best of the best.

Originating in Loganton, in southern Clinton County, Fishing Creek flows some fifteen miles before its confluence with Bald Eagle Creek. This fertile watershed is home to a diverse number of aquatic insects and has cold water temperatures supporting trout throughout the year.

In its upper reaches, there is a five-mile section restricted to trophy-trout regulations. This special-project area runs through an area known as "the narrows". Composed of riffles, deep runs and pools, the narrows is one of the most productive sections on the stream.

Access is easy, a well-maintained macadam road (County Route 2002) leaves the town of Lamar and parallels the stream the entire length of the special-project area. The land here along the stream is privately owned and one will find the area dotted with attractive cabins and fishing camps. Fortunately for all, the land owners, in cooperation with the Pennsylvania Fish Commission, allow public access for fishing. Parking can be found at roadside pull-offs. The combination of this extremely fertile piece of water and the special regulations has resulted in some heavy fishing pressure in recent years.

The trophy-trout regulations end just above the town of Lamar. For the next ten miles to the village of Mill Hall, the stream changes in character. It flattens out as it runs through fertile farm country, pools are longer, wider and deeper. The swift-moving currents of the narrows are now replaced with a slower more phlegmatic flow. This lower section is worth exploring as it receives less fishing pressure than the special-regulation area above. One should note that there is a section of stream near the village of Mackeyville that historically flows underground in the hot summer months of July and August, so don't be surprised, or discouraged, if you happen upon this area.

Access for the lower section of Fishing Creek can be had by following County Route 2004 which parallels the stream down to Mackeyville and from there State Route 64 continues to the village of Mill Hall and its confluence with Bald Eagle Creek.

If you like hatch matching, you'll be happy on Fishing Creek. Early-season mayfly hatches are almost always on schedule. Hendricksons, Quill Gordons and Blue Quills usher in the season while Blue Winged Olives and miscellaneous caddis show up sporadically. In May and June, Sulphurs are often accompanied by a good and eagerly awaited hatch of Green Drakes. We can't forget the prolific Slate Drakes and, of course, the fine summer and fall terrestrial fishing. We've never seen Tricos in the special-regulation area, but have had some good early morning Trico fishing in late August and early September on the lower sections of the stream.

Fall is by far our favorite time to fish Fishing Creek. September, October and into early November can be productive months. Most of the fishing pressure is gone, especially on weekdays, and there is something special about being out on a crisp fall afternoon with the mountains on fire with fall colors.

Memories come quickly to mind of standing knee deep in the narrows on a late November afternoon. We were casting streamers to likely looking areas convinced that any fishing would have to be subsurface. There were a few half-hearted follows, but things were pretty slow. We knew the season was about over and were just hoping for a few more casts before calling it a day.

Brown trout.

A handsome brown trout comes to net.

By mid-afternoon it started to snow, not a heavy snow but a soft steady fall of snowflakes that soon began to turn everything into a winter wonderland. I remember thinking that it was just about time to call it quits when Cathy pointed to the stream saying that she saw a rise. Then there was another one and another one. Bending over, we studied the water and saw the tiny sailboat wings of Blue Winged Olives. Cold fingers struggled with 7X tippets and size 20 imitations. For the next hour, we enjoyed what would truly be the last of the dry-fly fishing of the season.

Brook and brown trout are the dominate species in Fishing Creek. Before the spring of 1996, most of the fish in the narrows were from wild stock, but a late-winter flood let loose a large number of hatchery fish into the stream from the Pennsylvania Fish Commission hatchery located on the top of the special-project area. There are still good numbers of wild fish in the lower section, from Lamar downstream to Mill Hall, but this area also receives additional hatchery fish as well.

Fishing Creek has four tributaries that can also be productive fisheries. Cedar and Long Run are both limestoners that enter Fishing Creek below Mackeyville. Cedar is a small stream about 15 to 25 feet wide and offers some fine summer terrestrial fishing. Cedar also has a Trico hatch that's worth fishing. Long Run is the smaller of the two at about 15 feet wide, but like Cedar it too can offer the patient angler some good fishing. Little Fishing Creek is a small feeder that finds its way into Fishing Creek at the village of Lamar and Cherry Run is yet another small freestone stream that also supplies Fishing Creek and enters three miles above Lamar.

Most of Fishing Creek's "regulars" rely on light-line outfits for their fishing. Two-, 3-, and 4-weight lines will do the job (maybe a 5 for early season Woolly Buggers) and rod lengths of 7 to 8 1/2 feet are just fine. Wading in the special regulation area can be slippery so plan on wearing felt soles. Chest waders rather than hip boots will help you get around and will cover all fishing situations. A wading staff can also help, and don't forget insect repellent.

As we mentioned, expect to see other fishermen during the peak times of the season. Any stream this good and so easily accessible is going to get a lot of attention. The future of the fishing here will depend largely on the respect and common sense shown by the anglers to the property owners, please do your part.

Fall is a favorite time of year on Big Fishing Creek.

Blue-Ribbon Streams
Tulpehocken

One of the larger limestone streams in the state, the Tulpehocken is cooled by releases from the Blue Marsh Dam. Minutes from the busy pace of metropolitan Reading, Pennsylvania, this stream offers some unique angling opportunities. Along with the familiar mayfly hatches like Sulphurs, blue-winged olives and Tricos that you'd expect to find on any quality limestoner, there is also an abundance of caddisflies. This is a fertile stream with a good management program.

A 3.8-mile stretch of Delayed Harvest water below Blue Marsh Lake is restricted to artificial lures and flies only. Rainbow and brown fingerlings are stocked each fall and quickly grow to adult size in the cool limestone-rich water. With easy angler access and quality fishing, the Tulpehocken trout see a lot of anglers. These trout will often feed right next to you, however this is not to say they're easy, on the contrary they can be quite difficult. Because these trout are caught and released so often they soon become angler educated. It's said that most of the trout here have college degrees.

The caddis hatches are abundant and they can be difficult to match or imitate. Experience has taught us that most of the feeding activity is on the pupae stage so understanding caddis behavior is often critical to success. We found ourselves on a long flat piece of water on an early June morning. Tell-tale rise forms indicated that a fair number of fish were on the move. A good number of small sooty brown adult caddisflies were migrating upstream. Captured specimens were about a size 18 and our imitations looked like they would do the trick. Unfortunately for us, the trout thought otherwise.

Cast after cast came back unanswered. Our 6X tippets were lengthened, different caddis patterns were tried. The trout continued to feed undaunted by our presence. The rise forms were not the splashy kind often associated with caddis behavior, instead they like small gentle swirls and we thought for a minute that the fish might be taking midge pupae in the surface film but the adult caddis continued to show. Finally an insect net held just below the surface gave up the secret.

Spring-creek fly box.

Fly-fishing a Tulpehocken Creek caddis hatch.

Joe Macus and a nice eastern brown trout.

Brown trout.

Eight or ten small caddis pupae wiggled in the net. Tan in color with banded legs, one actually started to leave the shuck while we watched.

Our fly boxes contained a fair number of caddis pupae in various sizes and colors but none that came close to the real thing. In desperation I trimmed a size 18 Ausable Wulff down to almost nothing. First I removed the tail, then the white wings and finally I trimmed the grizzly and brown hackle leaving only a few fibers below the hook eye. Not much to look at but I was ready to try anything.

I'd like to tell you that the fly worked, that the fussy fish just ate it up. That we shared the one and only fly, that it saved the day. But to tell the truth, the fish continued to feed and they continued to ignore the customized Ausable Wulff and everything else. Our day ended with a lesson in humility and the desire to return and play the game again. As they say, that's why we call it fishing not catching.

Like most of Pennsylvania's trout water, the Tulpehocken can easily be fished with a 3- to a 5-weight outfit. Chest waders will allow better access to the water and be sure to have a couple spools of 6 and 7X tippet material. The trout of the Tulpehocken can be very leader savvy so go prepared.

There are plenty of side attractions for non-fishing companions. From shopping malls to famous Reading clothing outlets. Antique buffs will find plenty of shops to browse through. A good section of the land that borders the stream is within park boundaries and there are picnic areas, hiking trails and even a playground for the kids.

Lodging is available through nearby hotel chains and Tulpehocken Creek Outfitters (610-678-1899), can help with fly patterns and tackle.

The Little Lehigh: An Urban Jewel

Picture this, it's late January or early February and a light snow is falling, our thermometer reads a cold thirty degrees. Numb fingers struggle with 7X tippet material and ice periodically freezes our fly line in the guides. Anglers upstream and down of us share in the misery of the cold weather. Dimples show on the water surface as trout feed on minute midge pupae and adults. Our offerings, sometimes accepted, are more often than not refused as we try to imitate the midge activity. This hardy group of anglers share a passion for trout fishing. Some have traveled great distances for the day of fishing, others are locals who are more fortunate and live nearby.

And here we are. The stream is the Little Lehigh Spring Creek, located just west of Allentown. Under the stewardship of the Allentown Park System, the Little Lehigh is a true limestoner with a birthplace in eastern Berks County, near Topton Mountain. It continues downstream some twenty miles to the confluence with the Lehigh River in Allentown. Within this mileage are two special-regulation areas. The first is a Delayed Harvest, restricted to flies only, that starts at Lauderslager's Dam and runs upstream for approximately one mile.

The most popular, however, is easily found by taking the Cedar Crest Boulevard exit off Route 309 southbound, turning right off the exit and continuing to the first red light. A left turn at the light will put you on Fish Hatchery Road. Fish Hatchery Road parallels the Heritage Trout section, again restricted to fly-fishing-only regulations. This one-mile section of water supports an outstanding number of trout. Access is easy with two parking areas, one at the top or beginning of the project area, and another that falls somewhere in the middle of the section.

Most popular rivers have a loyal following of anglers who know all of the pools, riffles and runs. Anglers who show up regardless of weather or water conditions and who know the moods of the river. The Little Lehigh has quite a following, and at the top of the list is Rod Rohrbach. Ex-banker turned trout bum, Rod's life revolves around this wonderful spring creek

Urban fly-fishing on the Little Lehigh.

and its insect hatches. In May of 1993, Rohrbach made the fatal decision to open a fly shop on the banks of his river. These days, Rod spends most of his time selling flies and tackle and pointing customers to the better fishing areas.

Each summer the Little Lehigh regulars host a special day dedicated to honoring the late great angler, Jim Leisenring. Leisenring, considered the dean of the Broadheads in the early 1940s, published *The Art of Tying the Wet Fly*. His fly patterns had considerable influence on fly-fishermen in the Poconos and the Lehigh Valley.

Getting back to the river, the cold, the snow and the selective trout. Seeing the snow brings back memories of a different kind of day on the Little Lehigh for Barry. Twenty-five years ago, he was considered a regular of the river. Twice a week during the fall and winter, Barry would make the two-hour drive down Route 309 and make the turn on Fish Hatchery Road. It was mid-January and a storm was threatening, the thermometer dropping, any sensible angler would have stayed home. I said, any sensible angler. On the south side of the Blue Mountain, the rain turned to sleet. Well, Route 309 was really ugly and state trucks were out in force trying to deal with the snow and ice by the time his car found its way into the upper parking lot. Wind drove freezing rain on a horizontal plane and any normal person would have been two thirds of the way back home by this time. Undaunted and true to a very wide stubborn streak, he put a rod together and headed to the river. Actually the Little Lehigh had become a winter wonderland, the ground covered with new snow, the trees sparkled in the freezing rain, and for once he had the stream all to himself. Back then there was a swinging bridge that crossed the stream allowing anglers access to the hatchery side of the stream. On the far side of the bridge was a cement abutment and a path down to the edge of the water. Frozen fingers pushed the fly line and leader through the guides, and finally a size 24 midge pupa was attached to 7X tippet. He worked his way gingerly along the stream to the path. Well, one foot on that ice-covered path was all it took. SPLASH! The next instant he was sitting in the icy currents of the Little Lehigh. That path was slick as a whistle. Frozen pants, socks, hiking boots and a really mad angler made their way back to the car.

The fly-rod survived, the reel did not. Frame bent beyond repair, it would serve as testimony to the severity of the fall—but, it was not over yet. Highway crews were spreading salt on 309 as he slowly made his way home. The heater and defroster in his old Land Rover were turned on high, which wasn't much heat in those old Rovers. The

Little Lehigh River.

Pointing out a sipping rise on the Little Lehigh.

There's no wading permitted on this section of the Little Lehigh.

storm worsened and visibility was next to none. He kept chugging along determined to get home. The normal two-hour drive was headed toward four. When he got to the turn-off from Route 81 to Route 93 and home, he started to go into a skid and hit the brakes, he remembers the car sliding across the highway and onto the entrance ramp for Route 81. Now facing the wrong direction, and still sliding, he watched as a tractor trailer narrowly missed hitting the front of the Rover. When he finally stopped, he was off the road and sitting in a ditch. It would take four-wheel drive and a winch to get him back on the road and another hour of driving in four-wheel drive to get home. All this for a trout, a river, or both? The river fishes year around, if you can get there even in the worst of weather, you can almost always count on rising fish. For the most part, it will be midge fishing but there are dependable mayfly and caddis hatches.

If the special-project areas are crowded, there are alternatives. The open water sections of the river offer the angler a chance to fish over a healthy population of wild fish.

Tackle should be on the light side and if you like fishing 2-, 3- and 4-weight rods, this is the place to go. Our favorite is a 8-foot 9-inch Sage SLT series with a double-tapered 3-weight line. It handles all of the situations that we face, both on the special-project areas and the open water. A 9- to 10-foot tapered leader is sufficient and remember to keep your tippet

size compatible with your hook size. Tippets here will almost always be light since most of the flies that we use are from size 18 and smaller.

The Trico is, without question, the most popular hatch on the river, starting in July and continuing into October. This is a prolific hatch and will bring up the fish both on the special-project areas and on the open water. Terrestrial patterns like ants and beetles work well throughout the summer and fall season. Sulphurs show up in early May and last into mid-June while tiny blue-winged olives can show up anytime, especially on cloudy or overcast rainy days.

Midges are an everyday event, regardless of weather, water, or air temperature. Somewhere on the river the fish will be feeding on midges. No smart angler would think of going to this river without a selection of popular midge patterns that imitate all three stages of the life cycle; larva, pupa and adult. Caddis hatches will also provide some good fishing with both spotted and olive sedges active in April and May and the black caddis showing up in late July and continuing into early October.

It is truly amazing that this kind of quality fishery can exist in such an urban setting. There are problems to be sure, siltation continues to be a problem, development will always be a threat and yet this little limestoner continues to be a success story.

For more information on the Little Lehigh, contact Rod Rohrbach at the Little Lehigh Fly Shop, 610-797-5599.

Blue-Ribbon Streams
Penns Creek

If you're into aquatic insect hatches and selective trout, then Penns Creek is for you. Penns is one of the largest limestone fisheries in the state, equaled only by the Little Juniata. And, the incredible hatches, mayflies, caddisflies, stoneflies and midges, they're all there. In addition, a good portion of Penns Creek comes under special regulations. Access can be as easy as roadside parking next to the stream or, for the more adventurous, a walk into some of the remote areas where an angler can find solitude and rising trout.

Over the years, Penns Creek has hosted some of the best anglers in the fishing world, and still today has a devoted following of regulars like Bob Wayne, Fred Reese, Jim Hepner and Dan Shields who has published a River Journal on Penns. The late Vincent Marinaro was a frequent visitor as was Ernie Schwiebert. Charles Wetzel published his *Practical Fly Fishing* in the early 1940s and at that time was considered the dean emeritus of Penns Creek.

The stream emerges from a limestone cavern at Penns Cave, just north of the village of Spring Mills in Centre County.

The boat ride into Penns Cave is a commercial venture that is a favorite with tourists visiting the area. The stream is posted for the first five or six miles, but from Spring Mills downstream to the village of Coburn, anglers can find easy access to good fishing water. Access for the next 15 miles of water from Coburn downstream to Cherry Run is very limited. It's this section of water that historically offers the best in insect hatches and some of Penns Creek's largest trout reside here.

There is a road at Coburn that parallels the water for three miles downstream and ends at the entrance to an old railroad tunnel. From here anglers can walk following the railroad bed through the tunnel. Exiting the tunnel, anglers are now at the upper boundary of a 3.9-mile section of water that is restricted to no-kill, open to fishing year round using barbless, artificial flies and lures.

This remote section of water offers the visiting angler a sense of wildness that is hard to come by on most streams today. The water is wide here, sometimes as wide as 80 feet, and the stream bottom can be slick and treacherous. A wading

Undercut banks and fallen trees provide good cover.

staff can be a lifesaver. The Pennsylvania Fish Commission does not stock this area so the fish that are caught here are generally wild or an occasional migratory stocked fish. The lower end of the special-project water can be reached above the village of Weikert. Four miles east of town there is a well-used parking lot and a short walk will put you at the stream.

The Pennsylvania Fish Commission continues to stock Penns Creek below the catch-and-release area and downstream to the village of Glen Iron. In its lower reaches, summer water temperatures can become a problem as well as a healthy creek chub population that can be frustrating to the angler searching for trout. In the early season months of April and May, mayfly and caddisfly hatches bring trout to the surface and are eagerly awaited by the Penns Creek regulars. Hendricksons usually usher in the season followed by a Grannom caddis hatch that at times can remind one of a full-blown snow storm. Little blue quills, Quill Gordons and a variety of caddisflies round out the early season.

Mid season, late May and through June, one can expect March browns, gray foxes, blue-winged olives, stoneflies, prolific Sulphurs and, of course, the famous Penns Creek green drake hatch.

In July and August, the summer hatches are a mixed bag of caddis accompanied by yellow drakes, slate drakes and Tricos. Terrestrials always play an important role in a trout's diet at this time of year, so anglers should be prepared with a good selection of patterns.

September and October still offer slate drakes and blue wing olives as well as some good terrestrial fishing. If you're up to it, and can stand the cold, there is some good streamer fishing during the winter months. Patterns like Woolly Buggers and Clouser Minnows fished slow and deep can sometimes produce the largest trout of the year.

Fishing friends, Joe and Michelle Macus, traveled with us one June to Penns Creek in search of the Sulphur hatch. Fishing reports from other friends told of awesome Sulphur spinner falls and lots of good-size rising trout that were taking advantage of the helpless Sulphur spinners. The two-hour trip put us at the parking lot above Weikert on the catch-and-release area by mid morning.

We decided to walk upstream to a piece of water that Joe and Michelle were fond of. We spread out sharing the pool and started searching the water with a few different streamer patterns. After what seemed like hours of casting to likely looking spots without success, Michelle had a hit. Shortly after, a March brown dun appeared and soon others followed. We watched as dun after dun floated by, unmolested by the trout.

Then finally at the very end of the pool, Cathy saw a rise form. There was a partially submerged log laying parallel to the bank. The feeding fish was laying at the very head of the exposed log poking his nose out intercepting every dun that floated by. Cathy quickly cut off the weighted Woolly Bugger and added a section of 5X tippet and a size 12 March brown. It took just one cast to fool the feeding trout and in short order a handsome 13-inch wild brown was released. The pool went quiet so we decided to head back to the car for a late-afternoon lunch.

On the walk back, we shared our disappointment over the slow morning. After all, we had a pretty good hatch of March browns, but only one rising fish. When we first arrived in the morning the parking lot was all but empty, now there were five other cars and one more pulling in. The new angler parked his car and walked over in our direction. We noticed the Maryland tags and the TU sticker on his window. He inquired about the morning fishing, we explained our lack of success. He told us it was too early, that the Sulphurs would start around six or seven o'clock and go until dark. He said the hatch had been so good that he had made the long drive after work for the past three evenings. Throughout our late lunch, cars continued to fill the parking lot. Apparently other anglers were also well aware of the hatch. By six o'clock we were back on the stream and sure enough the Sulphurs appeared and so did the trout.

Now, we'd like to tell you of some great dry-fly fishing, of rising fish and matched hatches, but it was not to be. In the background we could heard a familiar rumble-thunder. It was soon accompanied by flashes of lightning. The downpour that hit soon after abruptly ended our fishing. Sympathetic friends told us later in the season that for the next week rain-free nights produced the best Sulphur fishing of the year. Sometimes it just goes that way.

For more information, contact Fly Fisher's Paradise, 2603 East College Ave., State College, PA 16801. 814-234-4189.

A healthy brown trout about to be released.

Blue-Ribbon Streams
Big Spring Creek

The spring creeks in Pennsylvania's Cumberland County are legendary among serious fly-fishermen everywhere. The Letort, Cedar Run, Green Spring, Yellow Breeches and Big Spring Creek are all at the top of the list.

This flat limestone belt is rich in many ways, the land that is still being farmed is fertile, crops of corn and wheat dot the landscape while the limestone springs give birth to cold mixed currents that travel alongside pockets of watercress and weed beds.

This is trout country, popular trout country, given evidence by the incredible number of out-of-state anglers that frequent favorite sections of water on any weekend of the Pennsylvania trout season. Maryland, New Jersey, New York, Virginia and Delaware license tags join the ranks of cars from our home state to fill the streamside parking areas.

It's Marinaro and Fox country, legendary anglers who developed the series of famous terrestrial fly patterns and who taught us how to handle the difficult fishing situations that exist here.

To say that we have a favorite stream would be difficult, we like them all. But, this past July we had the opportunity to spend a little extra time on Big Spring Creek. For a change, the weather cooperated, and as an added bonus, there was very little fishing pressure. In the three days that we spent there we saw very few fishermen.

Big Spring Creek can be reached by taking the Newville exit from Interstate 81. This will put you on Route 233 north, to an intersection with Route 11. Take a left on Route 11, and travel south for approximately two miles to Big Spring Road and a sign for the Pennsylvania Fish Commission Hatchery. Turn right on Big Spring Road and continue past the fish hatchery to the beginning of the Heritage Trout regulated water. This 1.1-mile section of water is maintained by the Pennsylvania Fish Commission and is restricted to artificial flies, barbless hooks only, and all fish must be returned to the water.

The upper end of the special regulation water is referred to by the locals as the "ditch". The ditch holds some enormous

Fly-fishing on the Big Spring Creek.

A picturesque pool complete with rising trout.

brook trout. In fact, some of the largest brook trout in the state are here as well as some respectable browns and rainbows. If you think brook trout are easy, guess again, these fish all have Ph.D's in selectivity and will challenge the skill of any angler.

The ditch is by far the most popular area to fish, there is a convenient parking area and a well-maintained bank from which to cast. The stream is narrow here and there's no need to wade so fishing in sneakers or low shoes is fine. Six and 7X tippets are the norm and tiny midge and terrestrial patterns work best on top. Underneath, cressbug imitations win hands down and some of the largest fish caught each season have succumbed to a well-tied cress bug. This is a great area

for a light 2- or 3-weight outfit, the casts are not long and the background is free and clear of trees or bushes.

For years there has been a lot of controversy and opinions on the regulated water below the ditch. Often described as barren of fish and silted in, the lower area sees fewer fishermen. Many anglers blame the fish hatchery itself for what they describe as a stream in decline because of the discharges from the hatchery. Others point to runoff from agricultural pesticides as the culprit. At any rate, prior to the construction of the hatchery, the stream had produced some very big trout. At one time, the state record was held by Don Martin in 1945, weighing in at 15 1/2 pounds.

Big Spring Creek access.

Wild brook trout were once common during Big Spring Creek's heyday.

On this trip we decided to explore some of the water below the ditch. Access was easy, with Route 3007 paralleling the stream for the length of the project. There are a number of well-marked and maintained parking areas provided by the fish commission. We stopped at the first one and sampled the fishing. It was obvious that we would need at least hip boots to get around here. The stream had widened and the banks were thick with weeds and cress. After an hour of fishing we had only spotted four fish, but one was a brown that looked close to 20 inches.

At the next downstream parking area, the water looked even better and after a short walk upstream we spotted rising fish. Seven to be exact and although they were probably only 10 to 12 inches long, they were there and were feeding on the surface. A final stop at the last parking area and a well-cast Letort Cricket produced the best fish of the day taken on the surface.

The more water we explored, the more fish we found. We didn't find as many fish in the lower water as we had up in the ditch, but on the other hand we had the stream to ourselves, rising fish, and the pleasant experience of a limestone spring creek.

While the fish in the ditch seemed to tolerate angler traffic, the fish in the lower section had the honed instincts of wild spring-creek trout, extremely shy and secretive. Most of the fish we caught had very dark backs which suggested they spent most of the time hiding or living beneath undercut banks and weed beds. The visiting angler would be wise to wear clothing that blends into the background colors and be cautious and patient with every approach.

A longer rod length was a real advantage for casting and for better line control on the lower water. Back casts were often long and traveled over high weeds and brush. Tapered leaders were extended out to 12 to 14 feet. The hot fly was the Letort Cricket fished in a size 14. Most of the rising fish responded and it worked well as a search pattern when we were just exploring likely looking areas. Like most spring creek fishing, a 3- or a 4-weight fly line will give anglers the required delicate presentation for these more-than-difficult situations.

The fishing in the ditch area holds up even through the winter months of January and February. Friends John and Chuck Ebeling make an annual New Year's Day pilgrimage to Big Spring Creek to kick off the new year in hopes of landing one of the large resident brook trout.

If you're a spring creek fan, then the Heritage Trout section of Pennsylvania's Big Spring Creek should be on your list of streams to visit.

Matching the hatch can often mean the difference between success and failure.

The Yellow Breeches

The Breeches, as it's fondly called by its band of regulars, has become a mecca for fly-fishermen not only from the Keystone State but throughout the mid-Atlantic region. Streamside parking lots are busy during the fishing season with cars sporting license tags from New York, New Jersey, Maryland, Delaware and Virginia. This Cumberland County limestoner shares its angling history with the famed Letort Spring Run, but stream personalities are worlds apart.

Unlike the Letort with its weed-choked channels, the Breeches reminds one of a freestone stream with a riffle/pool/riffle configuration and often mimics Pennsylvania's popular Penns Creek. Although anglers regularly refer to the Breeches as a limestone stream or spring creek, it carries a heavy influence of freestone water and like most freestone streams temperatures and water levels are affected by rainfall and air temperatures.

There are over twenty miles of fishable water on the Breeches and the Pennsylvania Fish Commission stocks most of it. The most popular stretch is the one-mile section of regulated water starting at the outlet of Boiling Springs Lake downstream to the end of the Allenberry Resort property. The rules here are catch-and-release, artificial only. If you are looking for solitude look elsewhere for this busy section of stream is often like Main Street at rush hour with no one directing traffic.

We recently spent an August evening on the Allenberry water with our friend Mike Schell, who lives in the Harrisburg area. Our plan was to meet in the Yellow Breeches Fly Shop parking lot. Mike had car problems and arrived late so we hurried into our gear and headed for the water. As we expected, the regulated water was busy with fishermen so we looked around for a spot where the three of us could fish together. It was not to be found, Mike finally managed to wade into a shallow riffle between two other anglers and after four or five casts was into a fish. In fact, upstream and down the majority of anglers were catching fish but this is not uncommon for this section of water.

A favorite section, "above the dam" on the Yellow Breeches.

Fly-fishing the little run between Boiling Springs Lake and the Breeches.

There are always plenty of fish here. Not only does the fish commission keep it well stocked, the Yellow Breeches Anglers, a local club which manages a cooperative trout hatchery stocks a fair number of larger trout giving anglers opportunities for fish over eighteen inches. Because of the no-kill regulations the fish caught are returned to the water. This social gathering of anglers as it often appears may turn some fishermen away, but if you don't mind the company there are a lot of fish to be caught.

The summer white fly hatch brings up every trout in the stream. The mating flight of evening spinners is dependable and predictable and after the white fly is over the terrestrial fishing lasts until the cold temperatures of late fall chill fingertips and toes. After that a slowly retrieved Woolly Bugger will produce results. Most anglers use smaller nymph patterns like Pheasant Tails and Hare's Ear's dead drifted along the bottom for success. Guide Tom Baltz, who knows every inch of the regulated water, has a few favorite scud patterns that he counts on to put his clients into fish.

Fishermen traveling with non-fishing companions will like the facilities at the Allenberry Resort which offers not only lodging but a tennis court, swimming pool and a dinner theater. For the angler, fishing is on the property, only a short walk from the resort. Hershey Park, the world-famous amusement and theme park, is nearby and there are shopping malls and restaurants to suit anyone's taste.

The Breeches for the most part is a medium-sized trout stream. The water at Allenberry is perhaps 50 feet wide but long casts are almost never necessary. Rod lengths and line weights while up to individual taste, are usually between 7 and 8 1/2 feet in length and carry 3- or 4-weight lines. The bottom can be slippery so felt soles are necessary and chest waders rather than hip boots will allow better access to the pools and especially the deeper water that lies above the dam at Allenberry.

While you're in the area, check out the little run that comes out of the lake at Boiling Springs and flows into the Breeches. It, too, has no-kill regulations and a short section just below the lake can be fished without wading. Don't bank on solitude here, like the Breeches it's a favorite spot for a lot of anglers. It's important to remember that the project water on the Breeches, including the little run, has no closed season. If you find quite a few fishermen around, try the water below the project downstream to Brandtsville. You may not find the numbers of fish here, but you will find plenty of room to move around.

There are two excellent fly shops in the area to help you with tackle selection, lodging suggestions or guide services. The Yellow Breeches Fly Shop is located on the banks of the lake at Boiling Springs, 717-258-6752, and Cold Spring Anglers is a short drive away at the edge of Carlisle, 717-245-2646. The fact that the Letort, Big Springs and Falling Springs are nearby is an extra bonus especially if the Breeches currents are running muddy from a heavy shower.

The Breeches was a favorite for Vince Marinaro and Charlie Fox. It's easy to see why after a visit. It's a pretty little stream and is easy to get to for anglers in the surrounding metropolitan areas. If you haven't tried the Breeches, put it on your list of places to visit. You'll be glad you did.

Spring Creek

Spring Creek is one of Pennsylvania's larger limestone streams. It is located in the central part of the state in Centre County and like most of our limestone watersheds, it is rich in angling history. This is George Harvey country, considered by many to be the dean of American fly-fishing. Having taught countless students the art of fly-fishing through his work at Penn State University, Harvey is one of an impressive list of fly-fishing personalities that have cast their offerings to the selective trout on Spring Creek.

Spring Creek also boasts of being one of the state's first trout streams to have a special-regulation section. The state dubbed the section Fisherman's Paradise and it quickly became a mecca for fly-fishermen. In the early days, anglers were allowed to harvest two trout per day and fishing was restricted to flies only. Anglers had to register at the entrance gate and there were limits on how many times you could visit the Paradise section in one season. Included in the Paradise project was a women-only section which was certainly the first of its kind.

The special regulations then included fishing hours. A siren would announce the start and end of the fishing day. The Paradise became so popular that the stream banks were lined from one end of the project to the other with anglers. Fortunately for everyone, wading was not permitted. The fish in those days were big, many of them came from both state and federal hatcheries. Anglers often left for home with trophy fish measuring well over twenty inches.

Today the Paradise section remains under special regulations but it is no longer stocked and most of the old hatchery breeders are gone. Regulations still restrict anglers from wading and a no-kill fly-only policy is enforced. Although the fishing is far from what it once was, the Paradise still sees a lot of pressure throughout the year.

In the late fifties, pollution from a number of sources including Keponne and Mirex chemical releases were devastating to the stream. The Pennsylvania Fish Commission eventually removed the stream from the stocking list and a total no-kill policy was established due to the health dangers of

Late-season fishing on Spring Creek.

Browns of all sizes are common here.

eating contaminated fish. Many anglers were ready to forget Spring Creek, but with time the water quality improved and amazingly today there are enough wild trout in the stream to earn a Class A trout status from the Pennsylvania Fish Commission.

Today Spring Creek offers many opportunities for the visiting angler. Its healthy limestone flows buffer against the acid problems that plague many freestone trout streams. A good portion of the stream has special regulations and most of the water is open to the public with easy access. The hatches are returning and the Sulphur hatch, in particular, is second to none. Tricos can be found on many sections and the midge fishing to rising trout can be quite challenging. Terrestrials work throughout the summer and fall months. Subsurface you can always count on small scud and bead head patterns. And, for the explorer, there are a number of tributaries feeding Spring Creek that are worth looking into.

On the average Spring Creek is about fifty feet wide and most sections can be waded with hip boots, although chest waders will allow for more flexibility. There is a nice mixture of flats and pocket water. Regular anglers rely on light 3- and 4-weight outfits, although opinions vary on rod length. There is a dedicated group of nymph fishermen who prefer the line mending advantages of a nine-foot rod while others choose shorter rods. In the end, it's up to the individual.

A favorite stretch starts at the Benner Springs trout hatchery and continues down stream to Fisherman's Paradise. This section contains a number of good fish and runs through property owned by the Rockview State Penitentiary. There is a well-maintained dirt road but only authorized vehicles are permitted, so most of the water is only accessible by walking in. The Paradise section is always worth fishing and there are shady areas and picnic tables which make it a popular place for non-fishing family members.

From Fisherman's Paradise downstream to the town of Bellefonte is some of the best water Spring Creek has to offer. This section flows through the backyards of streamside landowners but access is quite easy and well marked.

Lodging and dining can be found in Bellefonte. In the early days when the Paradise was in its prime, the old hotel in town was busy catering to anglers and their families traveling to the special-regulation area. Even today there is a section of stream not far from the hotel where huge trout rise to pellets thrown by visitors. This section is closed to fishing, but certainly worth a stop for a look at the fish.

If you're anxious to know the water and are short on time, hiring a guide is an excellent idea. A good guide will take you where the fish are, suggest fly patterns, and save you a lot of time in getting to know the stream and the area. Steve and Jackie Sywensky with partner Dan Shields own and operate Fly Fishers Paradise in State College. Their shop can provide a guide, tackle, and fishing advice. They can be reached at 814-234-4189.

The Little Juniata

David Ody led the way down the well-worn path to the Little Juniata. It was early afternoon and the heat of an early June sun found its way through the overhead canopy of oak and maple. The water looked in good shape and as we rigged leaders and tippets, David briefed Cathy and I on what we could expect in the way of hatches and fishing. Sulphurs and caddis were on the menu for the evening hours but the afternoon would probably be spent fishing Woolly Buggers and other search patterns close to the bottom.

The river was void of other fishermen, but David assured us that would change as evening drew closer. We spread out, each taking a section of water to cover. The cool currents felt good against the afternoon heat, the river was larger than I expected perhaps 100 feet wide from my vantage point and there was plenty of cover and depth to support a good trout population.

Rumors were there were some big fish in this water so I started with a larger size 6 Woolly Bugger tied with lead eyes to get the fly down quickly. Hours passed by as one

cast followed another, a sculpin replaced the Woolly Bugger but nothing I tried found any interest from Mr. Trout. A while later I found David and Cathy sitting on the bank where we first put in. Their report was better than mine, Cathy had two small browns and David had three, all taken on a small Hare's Ear Nymph. Skunked is not a word I fancy, but there was no disputing that in plain words it clearly described my afternoon fishing.

The sun was setting in the west as David was trying to convince me there really were fish in the section of stream that I had fished, so I returned to the same section with a renewed sense of optimism. I quickened my pace as car doors slammed announcing the arrival of other anglers.

The pool looked as quiet as when I'd left. Deciding that the riffle leading into the pool might be the best place to spend the last hour of light I moved into position and searched my fly box for a Sulphur dun. A thorax dressing caught my eye and as I attached it to my 6X tippet I heard more than saw the first rise. Mother Nature is full of surprises

Looking for a spinner fall in the evening light on the Little Juniata.

and for the next hour and a half I had fish rising everywhere. Sulphurs began to appear as if out of nowhere and at one point just at dark I had both duns and spinners on the water. Three other anglers had moved in below me and all of us had rising fish to work on.

It was hard to believe that this was the same piece of water that I had worked so hard on that very afternoon. I would be embarrassed to tell you just how hard those fish were to catch, but I ended the evening having landed 6 and losing another 3 but I should of had twice that many.

Flashlights were going on and off up and down the stream as the fishing ended. I met Cathy and David back at the car. "Well," David said, "do you still have any doubts about that fishless pool that you spent the afternoon in?" "Don't rub it," in I replied. For Cathy and I this was our first visit to the Little Juniata but I already knew that it would not be our last.

The Little Juniata is located in the counties of Blair and Huntingdon. Many Pennsylvania streams have had problems over the years with pollutants and the Little Juniata is no exception, but the future looks bright. One of the larger Pennsylvania trout streams, the Juniata offers diverse opportunities to the visiting angler from larger fast runs and riffles to long, slow-moving flats where trout set up and selectively sip in the evening mayfly spinners.

The most popular fishing areas are from the village of Tyrone downstream through Ironville, Birmingham, and on to where the Little Juniata meets the Frankstown Branch of the Juniata near Petersburg. Access is comparatively easy on the upper section of river by a secondary road reached from PA 453, that parallels the water downstream to Spruce Creek. The next four miles of water must be walked into. At Barree another secondary road parallels the water for the remaining five miles of the Little Juniata. There is no closed trout season.

Insect hatches on the river run from early season little blue quills to larger green drakes in late May. There are prolific caddis hatches throughout the season as well as a healthy crayfish population that undoubtedly helps support the larger trout in the river.

Tackle requirements may vary depending upon your taste, but the basic nine-foot fly rod for a four- or five-weight fly line will work just fine. Chest waders are recommended as well as felt soles. There are some slippery areas and runs that are swift and deep so be extra careful wading. A wading staff could also be useful in certain sections of the river.

Worth mentioning is the fact that Spruce Creek empties into the Little Juniata and although the majority of Spruce is private there is a section of water owned by Penn State that is open to the public. Spruce is a first-class limestone stream and a favorite haunt of President Jimmy Carter. Like the Little Juniata, Spruce has a number of prolific insect hatches including an outstanding Sulphur and Trico hatch. The Penn State section is regulated to artificial only and a catch-and-release program.

Lodging is conveniently found at various motels in Tyrone or the popular Spruce Creek Bed and Breakfast, located at Spruce Creek, 814-632-3777.

David Thieman releasing a brown trout.

Home Water: Our Fishing Creek

The old saying, "there's no place like home," is so true. In our work we travel a lot for Frontiers International hosting trips and for the Sage Rod Company presenting clinics and working at sport shows which also involves being away from home. But in between trips, shows and clinics, we return to our cabin home in the mountains of Pennsylvania. And, not far from our door is Fishing Creek.

It was here in this fertile valley that we fished as children. It was here that we landed our first trout, and come to think of it, it was here that we first met. Our life has always revolved around this valley and this trout stream. We hope it always will.

Pennsylvania has five Fishing Creeks. The most popular is in Clinton County, a limestone trout stream located in the central part of the state. Our Fishing Creek is a freestone stream in the northeast section of Columbia County. Two of the others are relatively close to these first two, and the last is in the Harrisburg area.

The great Iroquois Indian nation called our Fishing Creek, Namesesipong, or water with fish. We call it home. We take the clarity of the water for granted, but visiting anglers are often fooled when they find themselves in over their boots. Fishing Creek, especially in the upper reaches, is also very cold, and the stream supports a good trout population year around.

In its 29 of water, Fishing Creek offers a variety of fishing conditions. North Mountain gives birth to both the east and the west branches. The East Branch is acidic and supports only a meager brook trout population. The West Branch, on the other hand, is paradise for any brook trout fisherman.

Falling quickly from high on the mountain, the west branch is a maze of small pools and riffles that not only hold brook trout, but also a fair number of wild brown trout. The west branch settles down as it flattens out near the village of Elk Grove. For a short distance near the village of Central, it

Frank Matousek below Beishline's Dam on Fishing Creek.

historically goes underground in the hot summer months of July and August. It resurfaces just above Route 118 and joins the east branch about fifty yards below the highway bridge.

Beginning at the junction pool, where the east and west branches meet, iat one time was a state-regulated one-mile section of catch-and-release water. The upper half of this section has been damaged by years of flooding and bulldozer abuse, and the project has been discontinued. One mile below the catch and release area, the stream enters a boy scout reservation called Camp Levigne. This is a beautiful piece of water with easy public access at the camp parking lot. This area is best fished in the early spring or fall before and after camp is in session.

Continuing south about a mile on Route 487 from Camp Lavigne, is a dirt road to the right called Hackett Road. This road leads to a bridge and a small parking area. The water is good both above and below the bridge. Route 487 continues to parallel the stream as it finds its way to Beishline's Dam, near the Mill Race Golf and Camping Resort. This is the first impoundment on the stream. Below Beishline's Dam, the stream leaves the road and for the next mile runs south to the town of Benton. This piece of water can be fished by walk-in only and is worth the walk. It's a classic piece of freestone trout water offering solitude and pool/riffle/pool fishing.

It is on this stretch that as of his writing a delayed harvest regulated area is proposed. If this proposal goes through, Anglers will be able to access this water from the athletic field parking area at the Benton Elementary School.

Fishing Creek's character will change in the next ten miles as it continues through Benton downstream to the villages of Stillwater and Forks. The pools are wider and deeper given strength from tributaries like West Creek and Raven Creek. Public access is well marked by pull-offs and walk-in-only signs posted at various parking spots. This middle section of Fishing Creek is popular and sees a lot of fishermen. There is a private club that leases a half mile of water in the Stillwater area and the boundaries are clearly marked.

Below the village of Forks, Huntington Creek enters and has a major impact on the stream. In its headwaters, Huntington is a cold-water stream with a good trout population. But by the time it travels the 15-odd miles to the confluence with Fishing Creek, the water has warmed up to summer temperatures of 70 degrees or higher. During a drought year, this adversely affects Fishing Creek's water temperatures. This is not to say that the area from Forks downstream some 10 miles or more to the town of Lightstreet, near Interstate 80, is not worth fishing. On the contrary, early months of April and May offer excellent fishing. Route 487 still parallels the stream and access is fairly well marked.

The best insect activity is found from the Beishline Dam downstream to Lightstreet. Fishermen look to early season hatches of quill Gordons, Hendricksons, and little blue quills followed by mid-season March browns, gray foxes, slate drakes and Sulphurs. In the summer, evening

Falling leaves present a problem for Lefty Kreh on Fishing Creek.

The Stillwater Bridge is one of several covered bridges in the area. Below the bridge, John Ebeling spots a rising trout.

Freestone Streams: Our Fishing Creek

Cathy Beck with an 8-pound brown trout.

hatches of light Cahills and daytime terrestrial fishing can be excellent. The blue-winged olives in the fall complete the season.

Fall is our favorite season at home. Wood stoves are fired up and the valley carries the fragrance of burning oak and maple. The foliage is alive with color and the fall blue-winged olives show every afternoon. It's a fresh feeling to

be outdoors and the heat of summer is now but a memory. Along with the blue-winged olives come the ants. Swarms of winged flying ants that appear at random on the warmer fall afternoons. When you find them you're in for a special treat providing you have imitations with wings.

It was a windless early October day the kind that beckons you outdoors. We had a busy morning in the office getting a photo submission out to an impatient editor. The Fed-Ex driver arrived for our pick up and remarked that he was surprised to find us working instead of fishing. We watched the truck pull out of our driveway and decided that we should be fishing. Lunch would be a granola bar on the way to the stream.

We were headed for a long flat piece of water on Fishing Creek below the village of Stillwater. The pool, a favorite of ours, has a deeply undercut bank and plenty of overhanging hemlock limbs for shade and cover. The resident trout here are well educated by this time of the year and although you could almost always count on finding them, there were never any guarantees on success.

With fly rods rigged and 6X tippets we slipped into the tail of the flat. Upstream a heron lifted noiselessly out of the water. A fisher like us, the bird is a cunning predator. Wading carefully to avoid any tell-tail shock waves we moved into fishing positions. Fishing Creek is generally gin clear and clarity this day was no exception. With the help of polarized

Scenic Sullivan Falls on the east branch.

sunglasses we could see a number of good fish sitting tight on the bottom. The pool was unusually quiet and ten or fifteen minutes passed by before Cathy spotted a riser. I watched the fly line loop unfold as she delicately presented her fly. The take was almost undetectable, the fly simply disappeared and the fish was on. twelve inches of wild brown trout slipped out of the net and back to the water as I complemented Cathy on her fish.

Another hour passed and two more fish were landed, Cathy had worked her way upstream and was busy with a bank feeder when I saw the first ant resting on my arm. The light reflected off its cellophane-like wings. It had casters that were almost amber in color, tan legs and looked to be about a size 16. I knew from experience what would happen next and Mother Nature did not disappoint me.

Upstream Cathy waved and I knew that she was keyed in on the flying ants. Soon they were everywhere, on us and on the water. I remember thinking that if these guys could sting or bite we would be in big trouble. Smaller black-winged ants soon joined the larger amber-colored ants and the trout came out to take advantage of the buffet. This was easy pickings for the trout and we had swarming ants for about an hour. The last of the ants gone and the feeding frenzy over, we found ourselves sitting together on a log. Cathy looked at me and said she guessed we'd better thank the Fed-Ex driver. I agreed.

Tackle for our stream is easy. A basic 8- to 8 1/2-foot fly rod for a 3-, 4- or 5-weight line will do just fine. Chest waders with felt soles are an advantage for fishing below the town of Benton. The upper water including the West Branch can easily be fished with hip boots, but felt soles are still recommended. For flies, tackle, and general stream information, call Fishing Creek Angler, located just north of Benton, 570-925-2709. Lodging is also easy to find in the Fishing Creek Valley. We've listed a few for the visiting anglers:

The Inn at Turkey Hill, located at the intersection of I-80 and Route 487 (exit 35). Excellent accommodations and fine dinning. 570-387-1500 or Morning Dew Anglers in Berwick 570-759-3030. Fishing Creek Lodge, located about 5 miles north of Benton in Central offers rooms and breakfast (fresh from the bakery below). 570-925-5991 or 2681. There are several restaurants in town for lunch and early dinners.

Ricketts Glen State Park, a short drive from the fishing, offers spectacular hiking trails and water falls. Clean camp sites and cabins. 570-477-5675. Mill Race Golf and Camping resort has tent & trailer camping, and more rustic camping is available at Grassmere Park Campground, a small privately-owned campground on the upper end of the former catch-and-release area. 570-925-6655.

Come visit, we think you'll be glad you did!

Early season on Fishing Creek.

Freestone Streams
Pine Creek and Tributaries

As trout streams go in Pennsylvania, Pine Creek is one of the longest and perhaps best known. Seventy-five miles long, Pine flows through Potter, Tioga and Lycoming counties. In its infancy, Pine finds its way out of Potter County eventually growing in size from a trout stream to what is actually a river.

In its entirety, Pine has numerous personalities. The headwater sections offer the angler a quality wild-trout experience for both brook and brown trout. From the town of Galeton downstream to the Waterville area anglers can find both a wild and stocked trout population, and it is within this long and popular section of water that most anglers come to know Pine. Also included in this section is the Pennsylvania Grand Canyon, a rugged piece of water that is best accessed below the village of Ansonia and flows some 16 miles to the village of Blackwell.

This can be big water and in many cases because of the high vertical canyon walls is best accessed by raft or canoe. In the spring of the year, the rapids in the upper section of the canyon can be quite dangerous and a few people have lost their lives to the swift and forbidding currents.

From Waterville downstream to Pine Creek's confluence with the West Branch of the Susquehanna River, the stream becomes basically a smallmouth bass fishery because of the warm water, although there are certain areas where cold springs support a small number of trout.

Insect hatches on Pine Creek can be outstanding and just about every major mayfly hatch found in the East can be experienced on almost any section of the stream. A special evening in early May comes to mind when a favorite pool below Ansonia had so many Hendrickson spinners on the surface that it was impossible to find our imitations on the water, and we watched in awe as the evening light faded into darkness.

But it's more than Pine Creek itself that brings so many anglers to this north central area of Pennsylvania. Throughout Pine's vast mileage enter some of the best tributary trout streams in the state. There are so many, in fact, that it would take a dedicated angler more than one season to properly sample them all. Our two favorites are Slate and Cedar Run. Both are exceptionally cold-flowing freestone

Fishing an adult stonefly imitation on Little Pine Creek.

Fly-fishing on Slate Run, a tributary to Pine Creek.

trout streams that combined offer over 17 miles of scenic wild-trout fishing.

Cedar Run is a prime example of what a true mountain trout stream is all about, beautiful, picturesque, pristine, somewhat isolated and 7.2 miles of regulated trophy-trout water best describe Cedar. Waterfalls, pocket water, deep undercut ledges, laurel-studded banks and rising wild trout are just a few of the many reasons that we try to make an annual pilgrimage.

Cedar joins Pine Creek at the village of Cedar Run. Approximately 5 miles downstream of this junction Slate Run's cool currents mix with Pine at the village of Slate Run. Slate, like Cedar, offers a true wild-trout experience and has 6.5 miles of regulated heritage trout water instituted by the Pennsylvania Fish Commission. Slate is probably the more famous or better known of the two and certainly sees the most angling pressure. Under the special regulations, fishing is limited to no-kill, fly-fishing-only with barbless hooks.

State biologists tell us that Slate holds an impressive wild brown trout population. One can even hope to have a shot at a big fish here. Big here would be a fish over 16 inches. Now that may not be large by some standards, but on a small mountain freestone stream 16 inches or longer is quite impressive, especially when you remember that it's a wild fish. We never try to choose between Slate or Cedar, always making a point to allow enough time for both on our annual trip to the area.

Little Pine Creek enters Pine approximately 12 miles downstream of the village of Slate Run. Little Pine is a major tributary to Pine and it is anything but little with some areas as wide as 45 feet in many of its fishable sections. The headwaters start above the village of English Center and the first 2.5 miles of water are posted by a private fishing club. From the private club downstream to the 94-acre impoundment that becomes Little Pine Lake, the stream meanders through woods and open areas and is sometimes bordered by hunting and fishing camps.

Above the lake, the Pennsylvania Fish Commission has a one-mile section of water regulated as a Delayed Harvest program allowing artificial lures only. This section of stream is well stocked by the fish commission and consequently sees a lot of fishing pressure.

If you should plan a first visit to the Pine Creek Valley, we suggest locating at or near Slate or Cedar Run. By doing this you can easily fish one of the better sections of Pine itself and, in our opinion, the best tributaries that Pine has to offer are within easy reach.

Chest waders with felt soles are a must for Pine and Little Pine. Cedar and Slate can often be handled with hip boots but we generally wear chest waders for all of our fishing in the Pine Creek Valley. A nine-foot rod that carries a 5-weight line is the perfect outfit for Pine, but you should go prepared with both a floating and a sink-tip fly line. The smaller Cedar and Slate can easily be fished with a shorter 3- or 4-weight outfit.

In the spring of the year it's quill Gordons, Hendricksons and little blue quills that bring the trout in the Pine Creek Valley to the surface. Standard underwater search-type flies like the Clouser Deep Minnow or the black-and-olive Woolly Bugger are good bets as well as a deep-drifted Gold Ribbed Hare's Ear Nymph.

The Pine Creek Valley and its prolific tributaries offer many unique opportunities to the trout fisherman. We're sure that if you go once you will return. The Pine Creeks, Cedar and Slate Run areas can be reached by taking Route 44 north off of Route 220 near the town of Jersey Shore. Route 44 will parallel Pine Creek north through the village of Waterville where Little Pine enters the main stem of Pine. Just above Waterville Route 44 intersects with Route 414. At this point, 414 will take you up Pine and to the villages of Slate and Cedar Run.

Cedar Run Inn located near the junction of Cedar Run and Pine Creek and the Manor Hotel at Slate Run are perfect choices for lodging in the area. Both Inns offer a sense of country warmth and hospitality along with meals and both are within walking distance of Pine Creek. For reservations or information for Cedar Run Inn, call 570-353-6241. The phone number for Manor Hotel at Slate Run is 570-753-8551.

Tom and Deb Finkbinder own and operate Slate Run Tackle, a full-service Orvis shop in the village of Slate Run. They offer a guide service for the area and their fly bins are always well-stocked with fly patterns to cover the local hatches. They can be reached at 570-753-8551. Slate Run Tackle is always a favorite stop for us.

John Ebeling working a bank on Little Pine.

Cedar Run in Pennsylvania.

One could easily imagine this as a western setting. Big water, a drift boat, a heavy hatch and good-sized trout feeding on the surface. But, in reality, we are on the Delaware River, perhaps the finest trout water the East has to offer. The Delaware was not always a first-class trout fishery in its entirety. As a young boy, Barry fished the West Branch for smallmouth bass. The construction of the Cannonsville Dam, however, changed all that. With the cold-water releases, trout now flourish in the currents and eddies that once belonged to the smallmouth.

Our focus here will be on trout fishing in the section of the Delaware bordered by Pennsylvania. While the East Branch is also a superb trout fishery in its own right, and is also a tailwater fishery, it will be another story, another time. Not far below Hale's Eddy, the West Branch becomes the boundary for New York and Pennsylvania. Above this point, the river is bordered on both sides by the state of New York. Our fishing starts here on the Pennsylvania side of the West Branch. There is a secondary road that parallels the river here that leads down river to route 191, near Hancock.

One problem fishermen encounter on both the West Branch and the main stem is limited access. Fortunately, the Pennsylvania Game Commission owns a few miles of river frontage and has provided fishermen access and parking areas on this upper mileage—on the Pennsylvania side, of course. The next access, Balls Eddy, is below the Game Commission property and is owned and maintained by the Pennsylvania Fish Commission.

This is our favorite fishing area on the West Branch with good water above and below the parking area. Balls Eddy also offers a boat ramp and restroom facilities. The rest of the nearby water is clearly private and well posted, but remember once you are in the water you may move freely up and down the river. There is one final access area provided by the Pennsylvania Fish Commission off of Route 191 south, just below the bridge that crosses the river to Hancock, New York. This is a new access and puts the angler within reach of the Junction Pool where the East and West branches meet.

The West Branch is a very fertile piece of water and offers the angler most of the major northeastern mayfly and caddisfly

Upper Delaware River system; West Branch.

hatches. Most of the trout will be browns, but there are some fine rainbows, and even an occasional brook trout shows up.

In a sense the Junction Pool, as it is commonly and lovingly referred to by the regulars, is the birthplace of the Big D. The cold, fertile water of the West Branch helps create what is unarguably the best trout water the East has to offer. The river is too deep to wade in places with big pools extending beyond eyesight.

For many anglers the Delaware is intimidating, and it's not for everyone. From the Junction Pool downstream for the next 25 miles, serious trout anglers from the tri-state area and beyond come each season to pay homage to the river and its trout. Access from the Junction Pool down river to the village of Callicoon is extremely difficult to find. There is one Pennsylvania Access area near the village of Equinunk.

Many anglers choose to float the river by raft or canoe. The new angler to the river may do well by hiring a guide with a drift boat. Many of the guides have worked out arrangements for private access and there is no better way to learn the river and the hatches.

The hatches on the Delaware can be outstanding. We once witnessed a blanket hatch of Hendricksons that brought up every trout in the pool. There have been unbelievable spinner falls on the water above Equinunk and it's not uncommon for a giant rainbow to run well into the backing on the fly reel. Tackle needs to be taken seriously on the river. This is big

Steve Binnick on the Delaware River.

water and the experienced Delaware angler is most likely to use a graphite rod of nine feet in length and a 5-, 6- or even 7-weight line all have their place. Be ready for wind, it can always be a problem. Chest waders are a must as well as felt soles for better stability. A wading staff and a wading belt can be lifesavers, even for those who are usually sure-footed. Fly reels should have at least 100 yards of backing and a good drag system. While most of the trout will be browns in the honest 14- to 17-inch class, the opportunity to catch a trophy rainbow is always present and even a 17- or 18-inch bow will tax your tackle. These are wild fish, they can be cunning and shy and in most cases luck has nothing to do with success.

There are a number of options for lodging, camping and guiding services for the upper Delaware system. The Glenmorangie Lodge is a beautiful log lodge not far from the banks of the main river near Hancock. Starlight offers guiding and some of the finest lodging and dining in the area, phone 717-798-2350. Al Caucci's Delaware River Club offers camping, motel rooms, guiding, fly shop, and private river access on the West Branch, phone 717-635-5880. Lee Hartman's Indian Springs Camp offers lodging and guide services on the river, phone 215-679-5022. The West Branch Angler & Sportsman's Resort is located on the New York section of the West Branch and offers guide services on both the West Branch and the main stem of the river. They also have cabins and 3 miles of river frontage, phone 607-467-5565. And, if you're simply looking for

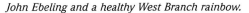

John Ebeling and a healthy West Branch rainbow.

A well-fed Delaware rainbow trout.

Main branch of the Delaware River.

a nice quiet room close to a good diner, call Smith's Motel, right outside Hancock, 607-637-2989.

When it comes to hatch information or what's happening on the main stem we always call Gene Ercolani at A.A. Outfitters in Blakeslee, PA. Blakeslee may seem like a long way from the Delaware, but Gene lives and breathes for the river and its hatches and no one knows it better. Give him a call at 570-643-8000.

For guiding only, we suggest the following private, licensed guides: Joe DePauw, phone 607-467-2217. Adrian LaSorte, phone 570-635-5968, and Roger Stewart, better known as Moose, phone 315-298-5763.

Keep in mind that if you are fishing water that is bordered by both New York and Pennsylvania, you may fish both sides of the West Branch and the main river with a valid New York or Pennsylvania fishing license. Remember, too, that once you're in the water you're free to wade up and down stream without being in violation of trespassing.

If you haven't explored the Delaware, perhaps this is the year to add it to your list!

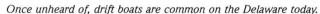

Once unheard of, drift boats are common on the Delaware today.

Stretching the day on the Delaware River.

The Lackawaxen River

Hendrickson duns floated by as the cold currents of the Lackawaxen pushed against my waders. The flat piece of water that my friend Norbert Tierpak and I were fishing looked productive but we had yet to see the first rise form. Norb who was about twenty yards above me held up his hands signaling his frustration. I had experienced this same dilemma of a heavy hatch but no rising trout a week earlier on the Delaware River near Hancock, New York. The water temperature was obviously warm enough for the bugs but not the trout.

I snipped off my Hendrickson dun and replaced it with a black Woolly Bugger thinking if the fish did not want to come to the surface and take advantage of Mother Nature's offerings, then I'd better put something on and search the bottom. The next hour went by without results, although I thought at one point I saw the flash of a fish behind my fly. My search with the Woolly Bugger had taken me down river and out of sight of Norbert. I switched to a sink-tip line and a slower retrieve and still no response from the trout, finally I packed it in and walked back to find Norbert sitting on the bank.

The Hendricksons were all but over as we talked of leaving and then I heard a splash that sounded like a feeding fish. We scanned the water and then saw not one but three different fish up. Cold hands fumbled as I hurried to switch back to a floating line. Norbert was quickly into a foot-long rainbow adding as he landed the fish that it took the dun on the first cast. I assumed that he was referring to a Hendrickson dun so I clinch knotted a size 14 Thorax Dun onto my 5X tippet and looked for a fish. I saw the nose as it broke the surface giving away the trout's position. My first ten casts were refused and I watched as the fish once more came up to a natural. It was at that point that I realized the duns I could see on the water appeared to be getting smaller. I captured one in my insect net but I already knew the answer to my question. A little blue quill hatch was in full swing and the fish were on them. Norbert landed another fish and I asked him what he was using, "A little blue quill," he replied and then he mumbled something about me finally figuring it out.

I laughed at his remark but thought how unusual it was to see the blue quills follow the Hendricksons, it's normally the other way around with the smaller flies hatching earlier in the day to be followed or sometimes hatching with the larger Hendricksons. I think often of the fishing we had that cold spring day on the Lackawaxen, it lasted almost to dark.

The Lackawaxen River begins in Wayne County flowing some twenty miles southeast to its junction with the Dyberry at Honesdale. Leaving Honesdale it travels south for another eight miles to Hawley where once more it picks up additional volume from Middle Creek. Below Lake Wallenpaupack the river turns in an easterly direction for approximately fifteen miles to its junction with the Delaware River at the town of Lackawaxen.

Access to the river can be found from US Route 6, which follows the river from the town of Honesdale down river to Hawley. From this point, access can be found from PA Route 590, and a secondary road that parallels the river. In its lower sections the water levels of the Lackawaxen are affected by releases from a P.P. & L. (Pennsylvania Power & Light Co.) power plant located above the town of Kimbles. P.P. & L. uses water from Lake Wallenpaupack which is eventually discharged back into the Lackawaxen. These water releases are unpredictable and levels can rise dramatically and wading during these releases can be very dangerous.

The best fishing occurs during the spring and early summer season. Water temperatures can warm by mid-summer pushing the trout into the mouths of cooler tributaries. Hatches include not only the more prolific mayfly species, but caddis and stoneflies as well. In its past history the Lackawaxen was known for a tremendous green drake hatch but years of floods and siltation have all but depleted this beautiful insect.

Waders are a must and felt soles or studs are strongly recommended. Nine-foot fly rods that carry a five- or six-weight line are the most popular and the wise angler will carry both floating and sink-tip fly lines. We rely on attractor patterns as well as hatch-matching patterns to fish the river and a selection of bead-head nymphs and Woolly Buggers should also be included. Lodging is available in and around Lake Wallenpaupack.

Lackawaxen River.

Freestone Streams
Kettle Creek

Whenever we hear Potter or Tioga county mentioned, we immediately think of whitetail deer camps, turkey hunters dressed in camo, wild brook trout streams and forests that seem to go on forever. There are bumper stickers on cars around these parts that hail Potter County as God's Country. There are trophy bucks here, rattlesnakes, and a healthy black bear population. The good hunting in this area brings hunters back each season. This is quite frankly still wild country.

Kettle is one of the most popular streams in the area and wild brook trout abound in the headwaters. There is much to explore here in one of the most scenic areas of the state. Kettle encompasses over thirty five miles of water and includes a number of tributaries that are equally famous.

If you like hatches you'll like Kettle. The early season trio of quill Gordons, Hendricksons, and blue quills bring Kettle's trout to the surface and the migration of Caddis often blanket the stream. Along with the smaller insects, Kettle still offers the larger green and brown drake hatches that have sorely disappeared from much of Pennsylvania's cold water. The most popular section of water is understandably the designated catch-and-release area that extends below the bridge on Route 144 and continues upstream for almost two miles. This section of stream sees a lot of angling pressure and is heavily stocked by the Pennsylvania Fish & Boat Commission.

If you long for a little solitude now and then, you'll find the upper sections of Kettle's wild-trout water attractive. You'll want to take a shorter rod and a selection of attractor patterns to catch these fish that offer more in beauty than in size. If you explore Kettle and its smaller tributaries anywhere above Ole Bull State Park, you can find a perfect combination of scenery, solitude, and wild trout.

Along with the pleasant fishing that Kettle has to offer, you may want to take advantage of Cross Forks and The Hammersley Fork, two of the more famous of the tributaries that feed into Kettle.

Cross Forks is managed by the Pennsylvania Fish & Boat Commission as a wild-trout stream. In other words, it is not stocked and the regulations on approximately 6 miles of the water are fly-fishing-only, barbless hooks, no-kill. Along with the wild brook trout you'll also be treated

A healthy Kettle Creek brown trout.

Releasing a Kettle Creek rainbow.

Bob Wayne hooking up on Kettle Creek.

water which the Pennsylvania Fish & Boat Commission keeps well stocked with trout. The Delayed Harvest area is located below the village of Warton, and sees the most angling pressure. Don't pass up the open water, it too offers some very good fishing. Like the other Potter County streams the early hatches bring the fish up and there are some wild fish in the upper reaches of the stream. In late May the fishing can be spectacular with blue-winged olives, gray foxes, and March browns hatching during the day and brown drakes, green drakes, Sulphurs, and slate drakes filling the air in the evening. Anglers can camp at Hemlock Campground near Wharton and at the Sinnemahoning State Park.

Access to Kettle and surrounding waters is pretty easy and the special regulations continue to improve the fishery. This is the perfect environment for the light-rod enthusiast and although chest waders are an advantage on parts of Kettle, most of the water can be fished with hip boots. Camping is available throughout the state park system. Go prepared to spend some time, there is a lot of water to explore.

Cathy Beck brings a nice brown trout to the net.

to browns averaging eight to ten inches long with an occasional twelve to fourteen inch fish landed. On small water that's a nice fish. Most of the stream flows through the Susquehannock State Forest so, like the upper Kettle, you're fishing in a very pristine environment.

The Hammersley Fork gets its start in the tranquillity of the Susquehannock State Forest. Like Cross Forks, the Hammersley is managed as a wild trout stream with no stocking from the state. Most of the fish caught here will be wild brook trout, although we've found a fair number of wild browns in the lower section of the stream. Access is basically walk in which results in light fishing pressure. If you're up to it, there are remote camp sites along the stream so the adventurous angler can hike in and spend the night. Another piece of water worth a look is the Nelson Branch, a tributary to the Hammersley Fork. Small in size but this little branch holds a population of wild brook trout.

We'll take one final look at Potter County with the First Fork of Sinnemahoning Creek. Located in the southwestern side of Potter County, First Fork offers over thirty miles of

Freestone Streams
The Brodheads

This Monroe County freestone stream, rich in fly-fishing heritage, is named after Captain Daniel Brodhead who negotiated for the land with the sons of William Penn in the early 1700s. Long before the Catskills became famous the Brodhead was hosting the best known of the fly-fishing fraternity. In the mid-1850s, actor Joseph Jefferson fished here with Thaddeus Norris, the father of American fly-fishing literature. Samuel Philippe (who is credited with inventing the modern bamboo rod construction), Buffalo Bill and Annie Oakley, and a host of others came to play the game on this legendary Pocono water. Sister rivers and smaller tributaries soon found their own fame as the sport grew.

Most stayed at the Henryville House, established in 1848, making it the oldest fishing hotel in America. As time passed, other lodging became available, but none as popular as Henryville. Fishing clubs began to form and eventually a lot of the water became private and remains so to this day.

Today Henryville is in the hands of a private club. The water there is as good as ever thanks to a proper stream-management program. The membership includes author Ernest Schwiebert, whose prose on our sport has delighted anglers the world over. His double volume *Trout* just may

be the best published work on the history and sport of trout fishing.

The open water available today is certainly worth fishing. The Pennsylvania Fish Commission keeps the water well stocked starting just above Analomink continuing down stream for about seven miles to Stroudsburg. Two tributary streams, the Pocono and McMichaels, join the Brodheads at Stroudsburg. Both of these streams have limited access but the areas that are open are stocked with trout.

Below town the river flows through a gorge with very limited access, but there is some great fishing here for the hearty anglers who find their way in to this section of river. The water is fast and treacherous and a sturdy wading staff is recommended. Below the gorge there is another stretch of pretty good water before the Brodheads meet with the Delaware river.

A few seasons ago we had the opportunity to fish on the Broadheads Forest and Stream club water with our friend Steve Binnick. The club controls water on the Brodheads as well as a section of the Paradise Branch of the main stem. Walking through the clubhouse was like walking back into time. Black-and-white images hang on old walls telling stories

Steve Binnick on the Brodheads.

of fishing adventures of long ago, and of recent times as well. The weathered walls in the tackle room held waders, boots, creels and miscellaneous tackle.

The water is classic Pennsylvania freestone, pools and riffles and wild brown trout rising under the cover of bankside trees. The fish were not at all easy and Steve solved the problem by matching the small midge adults on which the trout were feeding. Our best fish of the day, a healthy sixteen-inch brown, took Cathy's well-placed offering and pushed the 7X tippet to the limit. As we walked back to the car it was easy to imagine the ghostly figures of big Jim Leisenring swinging a brace of his favorite wet flies in the swift currents of the Brodheads or Arnold Gingrich casting one of his many Paul Young Midge rods.

Hatches on the Brodheads are as classic as the water itself. Early season mayflies like quill Gordons, little blue quills and Hendricksons arrive first followed by various caddis hatches that span the rest of the season. March browns, gray foxes and Sulphurs are on the water by mid-May and the slate drakes arrive by early June. Terrestrial fly patterns play an important role in the fly boxes of the regulars. Ants, beetles and inch worms are the game throughout the summer and fall months. In the fall, blue winged olive hatches bring the fish up and a well-fished streamer will move some of the larger resident browns. Chest waders allow anglers more access to much of the open water on the Brodheads and, as we mentioned, a wading staff, especially for the gorge. Lodging is available in nearby hotels and bed & breakfasts.

Ernie Schwiebert.

Brodheads Forest & Stream Club.

This is a stream without fame, a piece of water rarely mentioned by most Pennsylvania fishing writers. It's small water, not stocked in its upper reaches, and has no special regulations. However, it holds some special memories. Barry caught his first trout on a fly here on Huntington. It was a six-inch brook trout and being an excited nine year old, he quickly killed it. Well, after killing the fish he sat on the bank admiring his catch and started to feel guilty about the whole thing. The brook trout was just so pretty and the more he thought about it the worse he felt. He was soon crying and holding this dead fish and in the end he wrapped it in ferns and buried it. Somehow giving it a proper burial helped him feel a little better about the situation. The pool is still there and there are still a good number of six- and seven-inch brook trout that anxiously rise to a Royal Wulff or Humpy.

Huntington is a tributary to our home stream although our favorite water to fish is miles upstream of its confluence with Fishing Creek. Pennsylvania Route 118 crosses Huntingdon below Kittle, in Luzerne County, and soon after the stream enters State Game Lands #206. As it winds its way through the game land, it is at best a small wild brook trout stream and only accessible by walking in. The small pools have undercut banks offering excellent cover and the forest canopy keeps the water cold. A day spent here cleanses the soul of worldly concerns. One can smell the earth, feel the comfort of solitude, and catch a fish that has never seen a hatchery.

Below the state game land much of Huntington is private property. The stream increases in size as other smaller tributaries like Kitchen's Creek join in. Kitchen's Creek is stocked by the Pennsylvania Fish Commission but also has a good supply of wild brook trout. Although most of the fish caught are smaller wild fish, there are bigger fish around. Below the junction of Kitchen are some nice-sized brown trout who annually pull out of Huntington and find their way up Kitchen's to spawn in the fall of the year. Local turkey hunters have reported seeing browns up to twenty inches on spawning beds in late October and early November.

Warm summer water temperatures make most of the lower sections of Huntington too warm for trout, although there are a few spring holes that always hold a few fish until cooler fall temperatures bring relief. The only twin span of covered bridges in the nation stretch across lower Huntington Creek near the village of Forks. The bridges were constructed in 1884 for $720! There is a small community park at the bridges for public use and some good-looking water, but generally the fish are small smallmouth bass and creek chubs.

Hip boots are all that you need to fish the upper water and a shorter fly rod will allow easier access to the pools. These fish can be spooky so move slowly and keep a low profile. If you're lucky enough to be on the water after a summer thunder shower, a small black Woolly Bugger fished against the undercut banks can be absolutely deadly. There are a few nice browns mixed in with the wild brook trout and the perfect time to try for them is when the water is slightly off color.

Fishing Creek Lodge, a small bed & breakfast, is located about 5 miles north of Benton near the village of Central, 570-925-5991. There is camping nearby at private campgrounds and Ricketts Glen State Park. For flies and gear, stop at Fishing Creek Angler, about 4 miles north of Benton, just off Rt. 487, 570-925-2709.

An angler crouches on Huntington Creek.

Freestone Streams
Lackawanna

Imagine a river lost to the pollution of mine drainage and raw sewage, water not fit for any kind of life. That was the real story and the history of the Lackawanna. But today through efforts to clean up mine discharge and implement modern sewage systems the river has made a remarkable recovery. Located in the northeastern counties of Susquehanna, Wayne, and Lackawanna, the river begins at the outlet of Stillwater Lake in Susquehanna County and is an Army Corps of Engineers project.

A few years back John Randolph, the editor of *Fly Fisherman* Magazine, called and asked us to photograph the river for an upcoming piece that the magazine planned to run. This was certainly a surprise to us because at the time we were sure that the river could never support trout. We called our friend and fly-fisherman Jack Gantz who knows the area well and asked about the river. Jack asked if we had been living in the dark, we replied that we thought not. How wrong we were for not only does the river support trout it also has a wild-trout population and a trophy-trout project on over five miles of water.

Jack offered to give us a guided tour and a week later we were standing on a bridge overlooking a long flat near the town of Archbald. Directly below us we watched a pair of brown trout on a freshly-made spawning bed. The cool October afternoon was overcast and by three o'clock we were fishing to a hatch of small blue wing olives and rising fish.

The brown trout that we caught were not large but they were certainly pretty fish with golden yellow bellys and bright red spots, they reminded us of smaller browns that we see on Montana's Bighorn River. We spent the last hour sitting on the bank and listing to Jack tell us of the river's revival and the fact that along with the 10 to 12 inch fish that we had caught, the river also held a fair number of trophy size trout as well.

Access to the upper sections of the river is reached by Route 171, and an old railroad grade that parallels the river from Stillwater Lake down river to Forest City. At Forest City, 171 leaves the river but the railroad grade continues on to the village of Simpson and can be used but with some caution. Below Simpson the river flows through the populated town of Carbondale and it's hard to believe that here one can find wild brown trout rising to mayfly hatches. But the best fishing we are told is on the lower 5.2 miles of trophy trout water that begins at Archbald and ends near the town of Olyphant.

Jack Ganz on the Lackawanna River.

A beautiful fall day on the Lackawanna River.

We need to remember that for most of its length the river flows through numerous populated areas and you often find yourself fishing in someone's backyard. On the other hand the fishing's great. We spent some time looking at the stream bottom, examining rocks and finding a multitude of nymphs and larva, the bug life was impressive.

The river bottom is slippery and felt soles are a must, chest waders will get you to the fishing on the deeper sections although there were areas that we fished that easily could have been handled with hip boots. The average width of the river was probably 50 feet and its character is basically a combination of riffles and runs intertwined with pools and undercut banks. An eight-foot fly rod or longer with a four- or five-weight floating fly line will cover the bases. There are insect hatches, so go prepared to match the hatch, but know too that the many regulars on the river rely on small bead-head nymphs and black Woolly Buggers. There are numerous motels located along the river and finding overnight lodging is quite easy. If you visit the area you might also consider the smaller east and west branches of the Lackawanna. They both flow into the Stillwater Reservoir and each have wild brown and brook trout populations.

On our way home Jack said that he was surprised that we had not heard of the Lackawanna's success especially since it was less than an hour's drive from our home. We really had no answer other than the fact that he being our good friend had failed to tell us about it. With that Jack laughed and said now we knew.

Lackawanna brown trout.

Freestone Streams
Loyalsock

Pennsylvania's Lycoming and Sullivan counties have long been regarded as a sportsman's paradise offering a variety of outdoor activities. With a healthy population of white-tail deer, turkeys, and black bear, hunting plays a major role for those who frequent this mountainous north central area of the Keystone State.

Hiking and camping are also popular with miles and miles of well-maintained trails. One needs to walk only a few steps into the tall timber above the village of Forksville or hike a trail in Worlds End State Park to get a feel for being in the wild. Here you can still find a timber rattlesnake or hear the shrill call of a bobcat. There are locals who swear that mountain lions still exist here. But it's Loyalsock Creek and the fishing the area offers that brings anglers back each year.

The Loyalsock is a freestone trout stream beginning in Sullivan County near the small village of Lopez. In its journey downstream to the village of Forksville, the Loyalsock is a small creek. This section of water is affected by old mine drainage and the water here is slightly acidic. At Forksville, the Little Loyalsock enters and its more fertile currents influence the Loyalsock creating a sizable stream. It's 20 miles from this point downstream to the village of Barbours and this stretch offers a variety of access areas including the popular delayed harvest area. Below Barbours the water warms and becomes inhospitable to trout.

Like most special-regulation areas, the Delayed Harvest section of the Loyalsock receives fishing pressure. Yet on even the most crowded days one can find room to fish. Beginning at the Lycoming County line the special regulation area continues downstream approximately 1.4 miles to Sandy Bottom. This section is well-marked with Pennsylvania Fish Commission regulation signs stating it as delayed harvest, artificial lures and flies only.

PA Route 87 is a well-maintained road and parallels the Loyalsock from Forksville downstream to Montoursville and includes all of the best trout water making access easy. The drive along route 87 is worth the trip alone. The stream banks on the lower section of the Loyalsock are periodically lined with attractive cabins and fishing and hunting camps. The valley is rich in angling history. The late John and Richard Alden Knight knew well the Loyalsock's pools and riffles. Legendary angler Al Troth was a regular for many seasons before calling Montana home, and popular fishing writer Charles Meck writes lovingly of happy memories of the Loyalsock and its hatches.

Hoping for a winter trout on the Loyalsock.

Joe Macus winter fly-fishing.

The Loyalsock has most of the more popular mayfly and caddis hatches along with a fair number of stoneflies. Early season quill Gordons and blue quills are followed by Hendricksons and March browns. Gray foxes, Sulphurs and even an occasional green drake will bring the trout to the surface by early June. Tricos show up in late July, but we have found only marginal fishing to the hatch generally because of warm water temperatures.

Elk and Mill Creek are two tributaries that help cool the Loyalsock and both offer fine small-stream fishing. The Hoagland Branch is a tributary to Elk and it, too, has provided some great fishing over the years. Like Elk and Mill Creek, the Hoagland should not be overlooked by the visiting angler. A short drive on a dirt road from the Loyalsock is Hunters Lake. Owned and stocked with trout by the Pennsylvania Fish Commission, Hunters will offer a change of pace and can provide some great float tube or canoe opportunities.

Spring and fall are popular seasons on the Loyalsock, but we must admit that given a choice, the vivid colors of fall win out. There is something very special about an early morning drive through the Loyalsock valley with wood smoke rising from cabin chimneys and the fragrance of the burning wood fills the air. Size 20 blue-winged olives make their appearance by late morning and the chill of the cool mountain air makes one appreciate the warmth of neoprene waders. It's a special time in a special season and it makes you wish that fall in Pennsylvania and the Loyalsock valley would last longer.

The Loyalsock is still a fairly good-sized stream even in low water. For most of our fishing we use fly rods 8 1/2 or 9 feet in length that carry a 4- or 5-weight line. Waders are generally a must although hip boots are fine for fishing the tributaries like Elk and Hoagland. Popular mayfly and caddis imitations work fine during the major hatch periods but attractor patterns like Royal and Ausable Wulffs are very effective in the pocket water.

For those anglers who share an interest in both bow hunting and fly-fishing, the Loyalsock valley in the fall offers the opportunity for an early-morning hunt with the bow and fishing the afternoon blue-winged olives with the rod. The ever-popular Forksville Bow Festival takes place every fall at the Forksville Fair Grounds and brings in some of the best archers in the area to compete and display their skills at target shooting.

Camping and cabins are available through the Park Service at Worlds End State Park near Forksville and there is the Tannery House B & B located near the stream in the small village of Hillsgrove. Dennis Renninger owns and operates Renninger's Country Store in Hillsgrove as well as the B & B and can be reached at 570-924-3505. The store itself is unique and is indeed a true country store with almost anything from groceries and outdoor clothing to flies and tackle. It's all there. Dennis also guides part time and knows the Loyalsock and its tributaries like the back of his hand.

Dave Paden on the Loyalsock.

Neshannock Creek

One of the Pennsylvania Fish Commission's best management tools is the Delayed Harvest program. Limiting anglers to the use of artificial lures only, a limited harvest and season has provided anglers a quality fishing experience on streams that are marginal in their capacity to carry a healthy trout population.

Without going into great detail, the program goes something like this: Anglers must use artificial lures or flies and are allowed to harvest three trout per day between June 15 and Labor Day. Before June 15 and after Labor Day all fish must be released. The designated section is open to year-round fishing. And, the Pennsylvania Fish Commission does a superb job of keeping the Delayed Harvest sections well stocked with fish.

Neshannock Creek is located in western Pennsylvania counties of Lawrence and Mercer and offers trout anglers a very nice Delayed Harvest area. This 1.1 mile of regulated water sees a lot of angler use. It is an easy drive for anglers from eastern Ohio and for those in and around the Pittsburgh area. One can almost always count on catching fish and at times some really big fish. The Outdoor Shop in Volant is the local fly shop and gathering place. The shop sits on the banks

of a popular pool and anglers are often seen walking up to the shop from the stream in search of a better fly pattern. The shop along with the Pennsylvania Fish Commission makes sure there are plenty of big fish in the special-regulation area during most of the fishing season.

Angler access is easy and well marked along the project area, a hiking trail converted from an old railroad bed parallels the stream. For the convenience of anglers and shoppers, a pay-to-park area is located near the stream in the town of Volant. This is a popular tourist area and the town itself is worth a visit with charming antique shops, clothing boutiques, restaurants, and craft shops. Non-fishing companions can easily enjoy an afternoon in town while the angler in the family fishes.

Wading is allowed in the project area and the stream bottom is easy to wade. Felt soles are recommended though as it can be slippery. Most regulars prefer a four- or five-weight outfit for fishing the Neshannock with a floating line to handle nymphs, streamers, and dry flies. A five-weight sink-tip line might come in handy in the spring if the water is high and cold and you're chucking heavy streamers and nymphs, but these conditions won't last long. There is plenty of room to

Fishing on Neshannock Creek in the village of Volant.

A Neshannock Creek brown trout.

cast in much of the stretch and most anglers use a rod in the eight- to nine-foot range. If you venture down into the woods, of course a little shorter rod might be easier to manage.

The hatches start with early season caddis in April which can provide some of the first dry-fly fishing of the new season. A caddis pupa with just a touch of split shot teased on a cross-and-downstream swing can produce some very nice fish. The month of May offers some of the classics with Sulphurs, March browns, light Cahills, blue winged olives all arriving on the scene. There is even a nice brown drake hatch.

If summer water levels and temperatures permit, there can be fishing to slate drakes in the early morning hours and evening fishing to the white fly hatch. Terrestrials can also be relied on to produce surface action.

In between hatch periods, dead drifting a popular pattern like the Hare's Ear Nymph or a Pheasant Tail Nymph through one of the many runs on the Neshannock is a good bet as well as using a search pattern like the ever-dependable Woolly Bugger or a Clouser Minnow.

This is not always technical fishing. We watched one spring as a successful angler took a fish on almost every cast. It was one of those ugly gray days that blue-winged olives love. There were a few duns on the water but not much else and very little surface feeding from the trout. For our part we had one small brown between us. It had been slow going.

Finally we swallowed our pride and asked him what he was using. He smiled and stripped in his line to give us a look at the fly on the end of his leader. It wasn't much to look at, anglers who frequent the Paradise section of Spring Creek would have quickly recognized the well-chewed green cotton chenille Honey Bug. Don't know what it imitates but the trout like them. We thanked him for his help and walked away happily with two Honey Bugs that he left with us.

The story didn't have a happy ending. Armed and ready with the new flies we thought our luck was about to change and it did, it went straight down hill. After three or four casts we both lost our Honey Bugs when they got stuck on the bottom and the only thing that saved the day was a last-hour brown trout that inhaled a slowly retrieved black Woolly Bugger. They say fishing's not all about catching, but personally it makes a difference on most days.

Along with the Neshannock nearby Cool Spring Creek and Slippery Rock Creek also have Delayed Harvest Sections. Cool Spring is more of a medium-sized trout stream located in Mercer County. Slippery Rock in Lawrence and Butler Counties on the other hand is a much larger piece of water. The visiting angler could easily fish all three project areas in a long weekend.

Lodging is available through numerous B&Bs located in and around Volant. A valid resident or non-resident Pennsylvania fishing license and trout stamp is required. For further information contact the Outdoor Shop, Box 310, Main St., Volant, Pennsylvania 16156, or call the shop at 412-533-3212.

Pennsylvania's Smallmouth Paradise

Pennsylvania is blessed when it comes to fishing waters. Noted for its trout fishing and trout management programs, the keystone state is indeed a mecca for the fly-rodder in search of quality trout fishing.

But, many anglers don't know that Pennsylvania is also home to one of the best smallmouth fisheries in the East. The Susquehanna River is a fertile limestoner. From its birthplace in New York, the Susquehanna winds a four-hundred-mile course through Pennsylvania to its final destiny with Maryland's famed Chesapeake Bay.

The Susquehanna enters Pennsylvania near the north-central border town of Sayre and continues down river toward the city of Scranton. This upper mileage offers some fine fishing for the fly-rod enthusiast. Favorite destinations include access areas near the villages of Lacyville and Skinners Falls down to Tunkhannock. Wading is somewhat limited because of depth in certain areas, so a small John boat or canoe can be helpful for getting around.

For years this beautiful river fell to the misfortune of acid mine discharges starting in the Scranton area and continuing for some thirty-five miles almost to the town of Berwick. Here the river would slowly start to clean-up and once again become a valuable fishery. In recent years there has been a major effort to clean-up the pollution. These efforts have already made a big difference in the local fishing and will lead to a brighter future for this section of the river.

Our favorite section of the river begins at the town of Sunbury where the West Branch of the Susquehanna enters the main stem and continues some sixty miles south to the capital city of Harrisburg. This section of river reminds one of a gigantic spring creek. Large flats with weed beds and islands provide excellent habitat and cover for the smallmouth. Insects, crayfish and baitfish populations are outstanding here.

U.S. Route 11 parallels the entire section and the Pennsylvania Fish Commission has numerous well-marked boat ramps and access areas for the visiting angler. A boat is not always necessary because most of the river can be waded during years with normal water levels.

Anglers can camp at one of the many private campgrounds found along the river. There are a few motels between the villages of Liverpool and New Buffalo, but most of the accommodations are modest, at best.

John Ebeling on the Susquehanna River.

Toby Thompson with a smallmouth bass.

Pennsylvania Blue-Ribbon Fly-Fishing Guide

Smallmouth bass.

Clouser Crayfish.

From the Fibridam near Sunbury down river to the Holtwood Dam is a section of river governed by a Pennsylvania Fish Commission program called Big Bass. Under the Big Bass program, smallmouths must be 15 inches or longer before they can be killed, with a legal limit of four fish per day. Also, here and on all of the state smallmouth bass waters, is a closed season from the middle of April to the middle of June. It is by no coincidence that some of the largest smallmouth bass are caught each year within this special-regulated area. Here, too, because of the depth of the river and sometimes limited access, a boat can be a real advantage for fishing the special-regulation area.

Approximately ten miles below Holtwood, the river enters Maryland and continues its journey to the Chesapeake. Bob Clouser is the dean of the river here and needs little introduction to serious smallmouth anglers. Famous name-bearing fly patterns give testimony to Bob's ability to create flies that catch fish. The Clouser Deep Minnow, for example, will catch just about anything that has fins and swims. Lefty Kreh says it's the best underwater fly he's ever used. Bob, his wife Joan, and Bob, Jr., own and operate Clouser's Fly Shop located in Middletown, PA. Bob spends most of the season on the river guiding and instructing clients on smallmouth tactics.

A selection of Gaines Poppers and Clouser Crayfish.

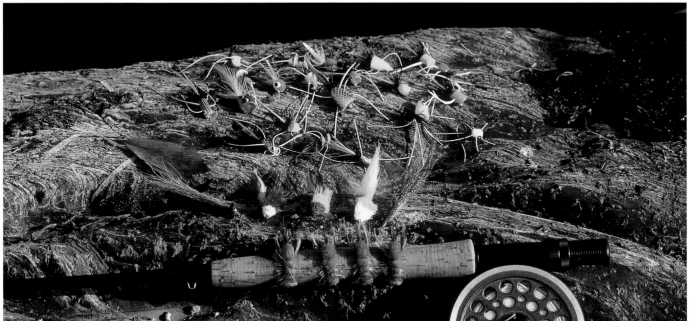

Every summer we try to spend a day or two with Bob or Bobby on the Susquehanna. It has always been a learning experience, although Cathy says she goes for the fried chicken and watermelon (their standard lunch). We know of no better way to learn about a river than to spend some time with a guide who makes his living on that particular river.

The Clousers know the Susquehanna, her moods, the insect hatches, and most of all know what it takes to catch smallmouth bass. Bob was the driving force behind the conservation efforts to put special regulations on the river and has received numerous awards for his efforts. He is quick to point out that the Susquehanna is without doubt the best smallmouth fishery in the East. Heck, he says, it just may be the best in the country. He may be right.

If you're a trout fisherman and have never caught a smallmouth bass, or bronzeback as they're often called, then you are in for a real treat. In the first place, most trout tactics will work for smallmouth. At times, they act very much like a trout. Feeding habits are similar and are affected by varying water temperatures. Like the trout, smallmouth will come to the surface to feed on insects. Like most predators, the smallmouth is an opportunist, often taking quick advantage of an easy meal.

Smallmouth bass are members of the sunfish family and spawn in the spring of the year. Quite colorful, the smallmouth has a bronze to brownish back and a continuous dorsal fin to the tail. Unlike its cousin, the largemouth bass with

Fly-fishing on the Susquehanna River.

Bob Clouser "Dean" of the Susquehanna River.

its bucket or oversized mouth, the smallmouth has a small mouth. Preferring cooler water temperatures of 60 to 70 degrees, smallmouth often share their habitat with trout.

We get excited about the visual experience of seeing the smallmouth suck in a surface fly. Popular patterns like pencil poppers or smaller hair bugs are great producers. But, the ultimate thrill for us is to encounter the summer white fly mayfly hatch. This hatch will blanket the water and if you hit it just right, every fish in the river will be up on the flies. A size 10 or 12 White Wulff works well. The smallmouth go on a feeding frenzy and it takes a little patience to pick out the rise forms of the larger fish when everything is up and feeding on the surface.

When the surface activity slows down, go back to an underwater search pattern. The Clouser Deep Minnow in black, tan, or white, or a Woolly Bugger in the same colors will almost always bring results. Because crayfish are high on the smallmouth food chain, a Clouser Crayfish fished dead drift along the bottom is also a sure winner. If you like nymph fishing, a stonefly nymph would be a good choice, again fished dead along the bottom. Most of the smallmouth flies that we use are tied on hook sizes that range from 4 through 10.

Weed beds are favorite areas to look for smallmouth, casting to the edges and retrieving flies back hopefully inducing a strike from Mr. Bass. Riffles and runs are fished best with underwater patterns either retrieved or fished dead drift. Flats are often the place to look for rising fish. It's on the flats that you want to be when a hatch is in progress. Our best dry-fly fishing has almost always been at dusk and often continues long after dark.

We prefer nine-foot graphite rods that handle either a seven- or eight-weight fly line. The advantage of the seven- and eight-weights are unmatched when it comes to casting a size-four Clouser Deep Minnow in the wind and the smallmouth is no wimp when it comes to fighting, if anything, he's a powerhouse. Fly reels must have a good drag and the capacity to hold at least a hundred yards of backing.

Most of our smallmouth fishing is done with a full floating fly line, but we always have an extra spool lined with a sink-tip that runs from slow to extra-fast sinking for those times when water levels force us to fish deep. Our average tapered leader for floating lines is nine feet, but quickly become three feet shorter with the sink-tips. Tippet sizes vary and should by compatible with the size of the fly used.

Never underestimate the smallmouth. He can be crafty and difficult, and when he wants to, he can tax your patience. We are often amazed at how many anglers overlook the smallmouth. We had two clients on the lower end of our local stream a year or two ago. We were fishing for trout and the surface action had been slow so we switched to underwater search patterns. In the course of fishing, one of the anglers hooked a fish that took off downstream in a huff. "Big fish," he called out to his friend. After a fight between fish and angler that lasted a good ten minutes, he looked down and said, "S____, it's only a bass." Inside his net was a beautiful sixteen-inch smallmouth. Only a smallmouth!, we thought. Gee, that's too bad! Here's a

Bass fishing on the Susquehanna River.

fish that put up a really good fight and so far it's the best fish of the day. So, we made a point of its beauty, strength and size.

At the end of the day, we were surprised to hear him boasting back at the shop about the great smallmouth he caught. And, he made sure all the other fishermen in the parking lot heard about his nice bass, too.

For more information on fishing the Susquehanna River or on smallmouth bass fishing, contact Bob Clouser at Clouser's Fly Shop, 101 Ulrich St., Middletown, PA 17057. 717-944-6541, or Dave Keck's Morning Dew Anglers, Rt. 93, Berwick, PA 18603. 570-759-1260.

Cathy Beck and Toby Thompson work a run on the Susquehanna.

Pennsylvania's
Still Water

Pennsylvania is blessed with water, historic water like the Brodheads and the Letort Spring Run with its finicky trout come quickly to mind. The mighty Susquehanna and the smallmouth bass fishing that it offers is known throughout the country. But only a few of the many anglers that visit the Keystone state are aware of the many Fish Commission lakes and ponds that offer a variety of fishing opportunities throughout the season.

There is no question about the popularity of running water. A trout stream or river is treasured to be sure with currents, eddies, and insect hatches. Even the sound of running water is exciting to the dedicated trout fisherman and most of us share an intimacy with the many moods of a river.

Still waters, meaning lakes and ponds, have character and moods too. Like many trout rivers, still waters also have seasonal changes, water temperatures rise and fall with fluctuations in air temperature. Weed growth affecting fish habitat and the ice of winter all have to be considered.

Most of Pennsylvania's state-owned lakes are warmwater resources offering some excellent bass and panfish opportunities. A few hold a carry-over trout population. Then there are lakes like Columbia County's Briar Creek Lake or Sullivan County's

Hunters Lake where seasonal trout stocking programs along with healthy bass and panfish numbers provide angling opportunities throughout the season. The Pennsylvania Fish and Boat Commission provides convenient and well-maintained boat launches on the state-owned lakes and all anglers must abide by the rules and regulations set forth by the Commission. Motors may be restricted to electric only and all boats using the state launches must be registered with the Commission. Coast Guard-approved personal floatation devices are required for each occupant on all types of water craft, including float tubes and pontoon boats which have become so popular with fly-fishermen.

Fly-fishing for trout in lakes can present new challenges that are not encountered in streams or rivers. Finding the fish can be the first challenge. There are no drift lines or stationary fish in lakes and ponds. There is no current to move the food so the fish have to move to find food. Generally the trout will be cruising at various depths looking for food. For example, the trout in Briar Creek Lake will cruise near the surface in late April and through most of the month of May. These fish feed on the lake's prolific midge hatches and on caddis pupae and adults that hatch during this time. With few mayflies present, the majority of feeding is on the midges and caddis.

Ralph Brunza fly-fishing on Briar Creek Lake.

Panfish are great for entry-level fishermen.

An angler starts the day on a Pennsylvania spring pond.

Another challenge for the angler is trying to determine which way the feeding fish is moving and where it'll show up next. By studying the rise forms, an angler will learn to make a good guess on the pattern and direction of a moving fish. As in moving water, casts should be made in front of the feeding fish. With this said, it's still true that too often you'll wait only to see that it has turned and taken a new direction, continuing to feed. Another cast, followed by another, with the same results and then your luck swings and for apparently no reason the feeding fish turns and takes your fly. That's lake fishing, at least on the surface.

Our favorite dry fly for this kind of fishing is often a small Parachute Adams dressed on a size 16 or 18 hook and tied with a hi-vis wing that's easy to see. The Adams can easily represent a cluster of small adult midges, a standard food item on which lake fish often feed.

Sink-tip or sinking fly lines can be a real advantage when the fish are not on the surface. We especially like the Stillwater taper offered by Scientific Anglers for those times when a slow-sinking line is needed. The Stillwater is crystal-clear and virtually invisible to the fish. Try working the shore line of lakes where the shallow water will harbor cruising fish. Searching these

Surface poppers for panfish and bass.

Lefty Kreh releases a nice brown trout on a Pennsylvania lake.

Pennsylvania Blue-Ribbon Fly-Fishing Guide

Ethan Blouin with his first bluegill on the fly.

Jack Ganz with a largemouth bass.

areas with Woolly Buggers and leech patterns often produce just about every species of fish the lake has to offer.

Lake fishing requires covering as much water as possible to find the fish. On Briar Creek Lake for instance you can work the entire south shore line by walking the edge and casting out to likely looking areas. A pair of hip boots or chest waders will allow you to do some wading and to get through the wet areas.

There is no question as to the value of a boat, canoe, or float tube for lakes and larger ponds. We think our canoe is just the ticket for being mobile. The canoe is quiet, giving us cover when we need to sneak up on cruising fish that are feeding on the surface, it's convenient to car top and easy for the two of us to handle.

Inflatable float tubes or one-man pontoon boats are also easy to travel with and to fish out of, and we see more and more of them being used in the state.

We also enjoy fly-fishing on smaller farm ponds for bass and panfish. Most of the time these are privately owned but, when asked, permission to fish is usually granted. Panfish are great fish for a new fly-fisherman—and the younger fisherman. Bluegills are not usually too sophisticated, they'll come to the surface to take a dry fly or popper and readily take a sunken nymph or wet fly. To make seeing the take easier, add a strike indicator. The indicator will float on top and dance around when the fish takes the fly. These underwater flies almost always provide action and results. Panfish are also good

fish to practice removing the hook from because they can be handled without fear of injury to the fish and inexperienced hands can keep them out of the water longer.

Fly rods of 8 1/2 to 9 feet in length are the most practical for most lake fishing. Line weights will depend on the species of fish. We like a 6-weight outfit to cover both trout, panfish and light bass. Our gear always includes spare reel spools lined with floating, sink-tip and Stillwater fly lines to cover any situation at the lake. Woolly Buggers, damsel and dragonfly patterns are good choices for underwater search patterns and a selection of dry flies and general nymphs should be carried for trout. Panfish eat just about anything, but a small surface popper is often our first choice. As the season progresses, fly-fishing for panfish really picks up as does the opportunity for a largemouth bass. Small mouse and frog patterns are popular choices for surface fishing. A largemouth bass will take advantage of any available cover so search areas with structure like fallen trees or stumps that are partially submerged or the edges of lily pads.

With the purchase of a fishing license, the Pennsylvania Fish And Boat Commission provides a comprehensive list of lakes within the commonwealth that are stocked with fish and a list of regulations governing the use of Fish And Boat Commission-owned or controlled property.

If you haven't tried fly-fishing in still water, you owe it to yourself to do it.

Fly-fishing in the fall.

Pennsylvania Blue-Ribbon Fly-Fishing Guide

Understanding Mayfly Hatches

Aquatic insects make up the bulk of a trout's diet, so it makes sense that the more we learn about what our friend the trout eats, the better prepared we will be to catch him.

There are four groups of insects that make up most of the trout's diet; mayflies, caddisflies, stoneflies, and midges. These are the foremost players, although lesser aquatic life forms as well as terrestrial or landborn insects also find their way to the trout's stomach.

Of all these insects, the mayfly is the genesis of fly-fishing. There are probably more dry-fly patterns that imitate or represent adult mayflies than any other insect. The mayfly is an ephemeral insect living in most cases for not more than a day or two in its final adult stage. It is a beneficial insect to all involved, the trout, the birds, and of course we fishermen. It does not bite or sting, and in its final adult stage it cannot eat. Its sole purpose is to mate and reproduce, fulfilling Mother Nature's intended destiny.

Many aquatic insects have what is called a complete metamorphosis; egg, larva, pupa and adult. The mayfly, however, has an incomplete metamorphosis having only an egg, nymph and adult. The mayfly spends the majority of its lifetime under water as a nymph. It breathes through a series of gills located on the abdomen. In most cases, the nymph will have three tails although there are a few that have just two. All mayfly nymphs have a single wing pad located over the thorax area. They have two feelers or antennae and six legs that are used for crawling along the stream bottom or for swimming.

In scientific language, mayflies have a Class, Order, Family, Subgenus and Species. There are hundreds of species of mayflies in North America. Now don't let that scare you, you're not going to need imitations of each one. In reality, fly-fishermen deal with about 14 or 15 major mayfly hatches through the entire trout season. Entry-level fly-fishermen are sometimes put off by the scientific and Latin names of the mayflies. These names are sometimes used by some seasoned anglers, but quite frankly, a trout couldn't care less whether a mayfly is an *Ephemerella subvaria* or *Paraleptophlebia adoptiva*. What he does care about is that the insect is available for dinner.

For sake of simplicity, fly-fishermen and fly-tiers over the years have given the major mayflies common names. These names are interesting and fun to learn. Sometimes they refer

Mayfly spinners can provide some of the best dry-fly fishing of the day.

to the color or size of the insect, blue-winged olive is a good example. Other times they reflect back to the fisherman who gave them the name, as in Quill Gordon. But, quill Gordon, blue quill, and March brown are names that you and I can easily pronounce, spell, and remember.

There is more good news, mayfly hatches occur on a calendar year. Hatches occur from early spring to late fall, so if we're prepared, we can show Mr. Trout a fly that looks like the real thing. Allowing for some minor fluctuation in weather patterns, the insect hatches occur at about the same time of year, every year. By using the chart below you can see that the quill Gordon hatches in early spring and that it is a size 14. As prepared anglers, in the spring we should have a few size 14 Quill Gordons in our fly box. And, that would include not just dry flies that imitates the adults, but a few Quill Gordon nymphs as well. That way if we encounter the hatch we'll be prepared to match it.

Having a few nymphs and duns (dry flies) for each hatch can amount to quite a few flies. There are a couple different ways to organize these flies. I have three separate fly boxes that I rely on for carrying my mayflies. One box is labeled early season, one is marked mid-season, and the third one is late season. In the boxes are imitations of the various stages of each mayfly that I might encounter on the stream. Carry two or three imitations of each stage of the hatch and you will have your bases covered.

With a little knowledge of the mayfly life cycle, it will be easier to identify what's taking place on the stream and what fly to choose.

Remember that the mayfly spends most of its life under water. That's important because it tells us that the nymph is available to hungry trout for most of the year, and it's why a good nymph fisherman is almost always successful. Mayfly nymphs live on the stream bottom, some borrow in the silt while others cling fast to rocks. Nymphs live on a diet of algae and dead plant matter.

For the better part of a year the mayfly nymph remains on the stream bottom. After about a year, Mother Nature calls and preparation for the emergence begins.

Most species of mayfly nymphs will swim toward the surface while molting, or shedding the nymphal skin. This skin, or shuck, will slide off the back of the insect as it struggles upward. The insect must free itself of the shuck in order to arrive safely on the surface as a winged adult. Other nymph species will crawl to the shoreline or to an exposed rock above the surface and once there will molt and transform into an adult. Sometimes, these dried, discarded shucks can be seen on the rocks alongside the stream.

The swimmers are extremely vulnerable to the trout for often in their quest to reach the surface they need to rest. In a suspended state, they drift helplessly along with the current and become an easy meal for a hungry trout. For the lucky nymphs that reach the surface, they must now break through the surface tension. Another struggle and yet another opportunity for the trout.

Obviously, a lot of insects don't get to be adults. Many will die or be eaten along the way. A hatch is when thousands of nymphs become active and start to emerge. A hatch can

last for a few hours or all day. It is indeed a lucky fisherman who is on the stream during a heavy hatch. The fish are enjoying a smorgasbord of insects and with the proper imitation, the fisherman will be a very happy person.

Once the surface tension is broken by the emerging nymph, the sailboat-like wings must dry before the adult, or dun, can leave the water. Again easy prey for the trout. For the fisherman, the insect is now visible and easy to identify.

Once airborne, the mayfly, in most cases, will look for a tree or streamside bush. There it will cling to the underside of a leaf or branch resting until it once more can shed its skin and become what is the final stage of its life cycle, the spinner. Generally the easiest way to identify the mayfly dun from the spinner is by the color of the wing. The dun's wings are usually a dull color. The spinner's wings are clear, almost cellophane-like in appearance and have a highly defined wing venation.

The adult spinners leave the protection of their streamside cover and gather over the water. This usually happens in the evening after sunset, or in some cases early to late morning, depending on the species. The male and female insects mate in the air and the female returns to the water to lay her eggs and die.

These eggs eventually become next year's emerging nymphs. The male may mate again, but it too will fall and die on the surface.

The now spent spinners lie flush in the film and may be hard to see by the inexperienced angler, but the trout see them quite well. Soft-sipping rise forms in late evening almost always indicate the trouy are eating spent spinners.

Learning about the aquatic insects that trout feed on can be fun and rewarding. Each stage of the mayfly life cycle—underwater, emergence, or on top—gives us a unique opportunity to fool the trout with our artificial flies. Imitating the insect and stage with proper color, size, and behavior is called "matching the hatch." Try it, it's fun.

Mayfly Hatch Chart

Common Name	Hook Size	Approx. Date
Blue-Winged Olive	16-18	4/10 to 5/10
Quill Gordon	12-14	4/15 to 5/15
Blue Quill	16-18	4/15 to 5/20
Hendrickson	12-14	4/20 to 5/20
March Brown	10-12	5/15 to 6/10
Gray Fox	14	5/20 to 6/20
Sulphur	16-18	5/20 to 6/25
Green Drake	8-10	5/30 to 6/15
Slate Drake	10-12	6/10 to 7/10
Lg. Blue-Winged Olive	14-16	6/10 to 6/30
Light Cahill	12-14	6/15 to 7/25
Cream Variant	10	6/20 to 7/20
Blue-Winged Olive	18	7/5 to 8/1
Tiny Blue-Winged Olive	22-24	9/1 to 10/29
Trico	22-24	8/1 to 10/5

Reading Trout Rise Forms

A feeding trout taking insects on or just under the surface of the water will create a disturbance. Anglers call these disturbances rise forms. Being able to spot rise forms and understanding them will make you a more successful angler.

Rise forms tell us two things. First, they help pinpoint the location of a feeding trout and secondly, they can give us an idea of the type of insect on which the trout is feeding. Your odds of success are instantly increased by fishing to a feeding fish and by showing it a fly that looks and acts like the naturals it's eating.

Over the years, fly-fishermen have given names to the various kinds of rise forms that a trout makes. Keeping it simple, let's start on the surface with what we will call the classic rise form. This rise form occurs when a trout quietly breaks the surface, takes an insect that is floating on the surface, and leaves behind a few circular rings accompanied by a tell-tail bubble or two. The

bubbles appear because the trout opens its mouth inhaling air, as well as the insect, and then expels the air through its gills. This kind of rise form tells us that the insect was probably sitting still on the surface, indicative of adult insects like the mayfly or sometimes an adult caddis, or even a floating terrestrial insect.

A splashy rise form is easy to see but sometimes hard to figure out. Because of the splashy disturbance on the water, it quickly gets our attention. Most likely, this type of behavior from the trout is the result of its pursuing a fleeing insect. Most anglers immediately think the trout has taken an insect that has been skittering, or moving, across the surface. But, be cautious and check for those air bubbles. If they are missing, the trout has probably taken a swimming insect just under the surface. When that happens, we need to retrieve and move our imitations under the surface and not on the surface. Emerging imitations of mayflies and caddis pupae are often

Rise form.

Tell-tale bubble.

the key for success in these situations. If, on the other hand, the air bubbles are evident then a skittering surface imitation should do the trick.

This subsurface kind of insect behavior is associated with many fast-swimming caddis pupae and some fast-swimming mayfly nymphs. Skittering surface activity is normally related to caddis adults.

The quiet, secretive sipping rise form is more often the most difficult to detect. Insects, especially tiny minute varieties, can be trapped in the surface film. Adult mayfly spinners as well as many midges, lay spent in the film and are easy prey for trout. The actual surface disturbance is little more than a small dimple.

This kind of feeding activity goes hand in hand with spring creeks where water currents slowly meander downstream through flats that are often home to ultra-selective trout. In these cases, only the very observant angler will succeed in fooling his quarry.

The late Vincent Marinaro in his informative book titled, *In the Ring of the Rise*, proclaimed that the sipping rise is an absolutely soundless, furtive, and the most conspicuous act in the entire catalog of a trout's eating habits. Marinaro goes on to explain that the sipping rise is deliberate and precise with the gentle tilting upward of the trout's mouth often so slow that the movement is almost imperceptible.

The head and tail rise form is also a quiet and deliberate act. Many aquatic insects, like mayfly nymphs and some caddis pupae, find themselves trapped below the surface tension. Here they often drift suspended for a time until they recover from the ordeal of swimming to the surface and can find the needed strength to penetrate through the surface tension to continue the transition into the adult insect stage.

In this situation, the trout have easy pickings for they often hold position just below the surface and with their nose slightly tilted upward, inhale the trapped insect. Often the back or dorsal fin and tail will break the surface as the fish takes in the insect and returns to the holding position. With this kind of feeding activity, a mayfly nymph or caddis pupa fished dead-drift an inch or two under the surface can be absolutely deadly.

Using a trailer is an easy way to act a small nymph or pupae just under the surface film to a rising trout. To the bend of a smaller dry fly that you can see, like a Parachute Adams, clinch knot a piece of tippet, usually 10-12 inches. I like to use 6X. To the tippet attach the nymph or pupae. When the fish takes the nymph, you'll see the dry fly go under. This is not necessary if you can easily see the fish when it rises but it can be very helpful in situations where it's more difficult to see the fish.

We have discussed feeding activity on or near the surface, but be aware of feeding activity under the surface and on the stream bottom. If conditions permit, depending on depth and clarity of the water, we can also key in on trout feeding in these areas.

It is not unusual for aquatic insects to get dislodged from the stream bottom and drift with the current until they reattach themselves to a rock or some form of bottom vegetation. When a trout moves to intercept the drifting insect, it'll often give away it's position to the observant angler. Its movement can often be detected by a flash of light reflected off its body. A skilled angler can see a trout sitting on the bottom when it inhales a drifting nymph. When you can see the trout holding in position, watch for its mouth to open and close. In clear water, look for profiles and confirm that you're looking at a trout. Don't be fooled by fork-tailed suckers. Watch the head and mouth for any sign of movement. With a little patience and practice, you'll actually see the white of its mouth, it will seem unbelievable.

When sight-fishing to trout on the bottom, place a weighted at the proper level and drifted right in front of its nose. Watch for the mouth to close and set the hook. Learn to look through the "windows" in the current and always use polarized sunglasses.

The more we learn about trout, the better our ratio for success. Understanding rise forms may take a little study and patience on your part, but it's worth the effort and will certainly make the game of trout fishing more productive and rewarding—which means more fun!

Brown trout.

Presentation:
The Key to Success

There are few things in the game of fly-fishing that are set in cement—generally there are exceptions for every rule. One rule without exception though is that you'll catch more fish with your fly in the water than you will with it out. So, keep your fly in the water.

Ask four of the best fly-casting instructors and you'll get four different opinions on how to cast. Talk to four fishing guides and they'll have four different opinions on the best place to fish. Ask a group of fly-fishing celebrities what they feel is the key to success in fly-fishing and once more, the opinions flow. Many put their money on the correct fly pattern, matching the hatch if you will, pointing out the importance of size, proportion, and color. Others point to the right time of day and consider water temperatures or the season. Finally there are those who feel presentation is the real key to success.

Success in catching fish is probably a combination of all of the above but when it comes right down to it, we agree on presentation. After all, you can be on the best trout stream in the world with feeding fish and the right light and weather conditions, you can have the right fly and the best equipment money can buy, but if you can't present the fly properly your day will probably end in frustration and failure.

Presentation includes more than just the cast. It's a package deal which includes how the fly behaves in the water after the cast is made, and in many cases, the angler's approach prior to the cast.

Sometimes, as fishermen, we don't pay enough attention to approach. On some streams, like the Little Lehigh in Allentown, the fish are used to seeing people. Here a steady stream of foot traffic from local anglers condition the fish. In this situation, approach may play a lesser role than on a stream that sees few fishermen. For instance, move on over to the legendary Letort Spring Creek in the Cumberland Valley, and the wild trout there are trigger-fast and ready to flee the instant an angler walks the bank. Approach tactics will vary from one stream to the next and sometimes even from one section of stream to another.

It's best to approach the water cautiously and use polarized sunglasses to locate fish that may be set up right in front of you. These are fish that you would have spooked if you had simply waded in and not looked ahead. Many anglers believe that all the fish are against the far bank and that's where they head, plunging in, sending shock waves ahead of them alerting every fish within range that danger is approaching.

Fish can hear very well, so avoid scraping metal wading cleats across a rocky bottom. Go slow, and keep a low profile. Many times it's your movement or silhouette that gives you away. By keeping a low profile you won't be as obvious. There will be times when you need to cast from a kneeling position to keep the fish from seeing you. Spring-creek fishermen used to say that if the knees aren't worn out on your hip boots, you can't be a very good fisherman. Wear clothing that blends in with the background, most often greens and browns on trout streams. Learn to think and act like a predator. The great blue heron is a perfect example when it comes to stealth and cunning. We can learn much from nature and this bird is a great teacher. A heron moves slowly, always alert and always looking ahead, always patient and camouflaged, as it quietly stalks its prey. Try to do the same.

Your cast should be an indication of the conditions in which you're fishing. When fishing flat, calm, clear water, these conditions warrant a gentle presentation, allowing the fly, leader, and line to land on the water as quietly as possible. Fish in these conditions, regardless of species, are generally high strung and ready to spook at the slightest sign of danger. A cast that comes crashing down on the water will surely do just that. Keep in mind that lighter fly lines and longer leaders are generally an advantage under these tough conditions.

A carefully executed cast on the Letort.

High forward casts on a sunny day will often throw shadows across the bottom, spooking the fish. Shadows alert the fish to danger from above—an osprey, kingfisher, or heron. Use a side arm cast keeping it low and close to the water. If the surface is choppy, the chop may work to your advantage allowing you to get closer to the fish. In these conditions, presentation may not be as critical as on flat calm water.

Get your fly to the fish as quickly as you can. While it may be fun to false cast, the most efficient presentation will be made with a minimum of false casts. Accuracy is important, too. If a fish is cruising, get your fly ahead of the fish so the fish can see it. But, when the fish is stationary in calm water, twitch or skitter the fly out in front of the fish to get its attention without spooking him.

If your fly is a streamer pattern that imitates smaller baitfish, remember that smaller fish never attack larger fish (or a least not more than once)! Retrieve your streamer so the fish sees it and, hopefully, will think it's an easy dinner. Don't retrieve it towards the fish, but away from it, off to the side so that he can spot it. When the fish sees the fly, speed-up or make longer retrieves so the fish thinks that his dinner is slipping away. Little fish being pursued by bigger fish don't ever slow down!

Drag in moving water will present problems. Mayflies, caddisflies, larvae, and many terrestrial insects that trout feed on will often drift with the current speed both on the surface and below. Fly fishermen refer to this as a dead drift, the insect is simply moving along with the current. Our imitation needs to mimic the behavior of the natural. Unfortunately, our fly is attached to a leader and if we put tension on the line and leader, it immediately puts drag on the fly and it will no longer ride with the current speed as does the natural. A smart fish will always be suspicious of flies that have drag.

If your dry fly or strike indicator is traveling downstream faster than other insects or floating objects on the surface, then you surely have unwanted tension on the line and leader. By adding a controlled amount of slack in your cast, the fly will drift more naturally with the current speed and look more like the real thing to the fish.

The first mistake many anglers make after the cast is made is to raise the rod tip. This immediately pulls in line and creates tension on the cast. After the cast is made, keep the rod tip at or below waist level. And, as the current carries the line and fly downstream, move the rod tip along with it so the tip doesn't put tension on the fly.

Mending or adding slack to the system as the fly goes through the drift is a technique that every angler should master. When mending the cast, don't move the fly. Use slack line from your line hand to mend with and make the mend as soon as the line is on the water for best results.

Imitating insect behavior may also mean that at times you need to skate or move your dry fly across the surface. Many caddisflies skitter, so movement in this case is necessary. The same goes for imitating emerging insects like caddis pupae or mayfly nymphs that are swimming to the surface. Do whatever you can to ensure that your fly imitates the natural insect.

Covering a fish on Penns Creek.

Noise can sometimes create interest, especially when bass fishing with surface poppers. This may sound like we're breaking all the rules, but a well-placed surface popper landing next to likely looking cover or structure and then retrieved in a succession of loud pops can really turn a fish on. Not only bass but most panfish and pike, as well, are attracted by the noise poppers make. Normally shy and suspicious, trout that refuse tiny offerings on size-24 hooks, will charge a noisy, squirming grasshopper and inhale the fly like there is no tomorrow. Like we said, there are exceptions to almost every rule.

Obviously none of the above techniques work unless you can cast and good casting only comes from practice. People who are good at golf, tennis, bowling, and so on are good because they practice, fly-casters need to do the same.

If you're new to the game, get some help, nothing beats hands-on instruction. If that's not possible, then a casting video by a well-known instructor can help. Practice laying the line down gently, set up targets and practice your accuracy, remember to keep your rod tip down and work on mending line and adding controlled slack.

Certainly it helps to have the right fly pattern, but it's only one piece of the puzzle. You also have to *present* it to the fish the way the fish wants to see it.

Fishing Nymphs

Fish do most of their feeding under the surface. Therefore, it makes sense that flies fished subsurface will be more productive overall for the angler. Make no mistake about it, we love to fish dry flies and will quickly agree that a visual strike on the surface is really exciting. But, the odds are stacked with the flies that imitate baitfish or the underwater stages of aquatic insects.

We generally refer to the angler who is fishing subsurface with imitations of aquatic insects as a nymph fisherman. Nymph fishing is a true art form in itself. A good nymph fisherman can be deadly, literally. He's put in his time, honed his skills, and has developed a hair-trigger strike.

A good nymph fisherman will also understand the life cycles and behavior patterns of all the underwater aquatic insects that fish feed upon. Mayfly and stonefly nymphs, caddis, midge larvae and pupae stages, and in certain rivers aquatic worms all play an important role in a trout's diet.

There are times when the nymph fisherman needs to be imitating a drifting insect and other times a swimming insect. If a mayfly or stonefly nymph is dislodged from the stream bottom, it may float in the current for some distance until it can cling fast to another rock or some form of vegetation. This drifting insect is a sitting duck for the always-hungry trout.

For the inexperienced fly-fisherman, the dead-drifting of an insect with the current speed can be hard to imitate. It's important to remember that the real insect is unattached and will drift freely, so our imitation must imitate that same drag-free drift.

Drag, is the term fly-fishermen use for unwanted tension on the line, leader and fly and can make your imitation look unnatural to the wary trout. Drag on a dry-fly floating on the surface can often be detected by the angler and can usually be corrected by various means of line mending. But, subsurface drag is often undetectable and drift after drift can be made without results.

Controlled slack in the fly line and leader is the answer, but the key word here is controlled. Too much slack and you will never be able to detect the strike, not enough will result in unwanted drag. There are a lot of serious nymph fishermen who feel that the more fly line on the water the better the

Sam Battaglino selects a nymph on Fishing Creek.

Winter fish will often take nymphs fished deep.

chances are of getting unwanted drag. The answer to line control is to fish a fairly long leader (9 to 15 feet) with as little fly line on the water as possible.

To achieve this the angler should make a short quartering upstream cast, holding the rod tip high in a slightly off vertical position. The rod tip should follow the direction of the drift until the fly has passed the angler. At this point the rod tip is slowly lowered, tension is picked up on the fly line and the fly swings from the bottom toward the surface. This swing can imitate an emerging insect. At the end of the swing, the rod tip is slowly lifted and the quartering upstream cast is slowly repeated.

This is tight-in fishing, most casts are no more than twenty feet and the angler must pay acute attention to the end of the fly line from the time it hits the water until the end of the drift. The fish can take the fly at any time.

Using the technique of a short line, long leader, and high rod tip is often referred to as high-sticking. The fly needs to sink quickly, so the flies are often weighted or split shot is attached to the leader to help get it quickly to the bottom. Using a vertical curve or tuck cast is an advantage in getting a lot of slack in the cast immediately upon contact with the water, allowing the fly to start sinking instantly. High-sticking can be absolutely deadly in the right angler's hands.

With the line under control you can cover almost every inch of available stream bottom working thoroughly and slowly, cast after cast, putting your fly on the bottom and often right on the trout's nose.

A strike indicator can also be an asset. These visual aids help detect strikes, but you must remember to re-adjust the indicator as water levels change. For instance, if you start at the head of a run which tails out into a deeper pool, you'll have to adjust your strike indicator for deeper water as the depth changes. And, the amount of weight on the leader may also have to be re-adjusted. More weight will be needed for deeper water and less for shallow water.

One of the best high-stickers on our home stream, Fishing Creek, is Ron Poles. Ron was a professional guide whose clients rarely went fishless. We made the mistake one day of fishing behind him through a favorite pool. As we fished along together, it seemed like he had a fish about every five minutes. At the end of the pool the count went 9 for him, 3 for us.

When we met up, we had two questions for him. First, exactly what fly was he using, and secondly, doesn't his arm get tired from holding up the rod tip. Grinning, he laughed and held back on both answers. After a minute of rubbing it in, he handed over a well-chewed Hare's Ear Nymph. The secret was not so much in the fly pattern this particular day, but getting it down to where the fish were and having total control of the drift. Add to that the fact that Ron is very patient and concentrates on every cast. High-sticking is certainly not limited to just trout fishing. Bob Clouser, the dean of the Susquehanna, and rightfully called Mr. Smallmouth, uses the high-sticking technique very effectively to put his Clouser Crayfish imitations right on the bottom—and does it ever work! We spent a day with Bob and watched over forty smallmouth succumb to a well-drifted Clouser Crayfish. Bob will tell you that there are times when you have to hit them on the nose. He made believers out of us.

Most high-stickers like longer fly rods feeling that the length helps with line control. The most popular rod lengths are from 9 to 10 feet. Fly-ine weights vary from one angler to the next, but a floating 4 or 5 weight normally fills the bill. Fly-line color is always debated, but most agree on a highly visible line that can be easily seen.

Popular fly patterns that match underwater stages of aquatic insects should be fished in and around peak hatch periods. We're not suggesting that you should be high-sticking on the bottom when the trout are rising on the surface, but rather around hatch periods when there is no activity on the surface. A Woolly Bugger can be extremely effective fished dead-drift on the bottom for either trout or smallmouth bass and yet most fly-fishermen never think to do anything but retrieve this pattern.

High-sticking may not be for everyone, but master the technique and it will increase your numbers of fish caught.

Headwaters of Fishing Creek.